A Bowl of Red

*Being a Natural History of Chili con Carne
and Other Native Foods of the Southwest, with Recipes
and a Guide to Paper Napkin Restaurants.*

Frank X. Tolbert
A Bowl of Red

Taylor Publishing Company
Dallas, Texas

Publisher's Note: due to *A Bowl of Red's* stature as a classic in its field, no attempt has been made to alter any factual details or personal views which may have become outdated since its first publication in 1953.

Published by Taylor Publishing Company
1550 West Mockingbird Lane
Dallas, Texas 75235
All rights reserved.
No part of this book may be reproduced in any form
without written permission from the publisher.

Library of Congress Cataloging-in-Publication Data

The Library of Congress catalogued the first printing
of this title as follows:

Tolbert, Frank X.
A bowl of red [by] Frank X. Tolbert, Garden City,
N.Y., Doubleday, 1972.
viii, 205 p. 22 cm. $5.95
1. Chili con carne. 2. Cookery, American —
Southwestern States.
I. Title.
TX633.T64 1972 641.8'2 72-85364
ISBN 0-385-18182-5 MARC
Library of Congress 72 [4]
ISBN: 0-87833-652-4 (Taylor Publishing Company
assignment)

Printed in the United States of America

10   9   8   7   6   5   4   3   2   1

To three early delvers in "chili history,"
O. Henry, E. DeGolyer, and Joe Cooper,
and with the wish that they'd all lived to
join the Chili Appreciation Society (International).

Contents

A Bowl of Red

Prologue

"Cowboys today is mostly a crowd of sissies."
Cap Warren, range cook
of the Waggoner Ranch

"If you do it right, grinding up them eye-watering peppers and dicing the beef, chili is lots of bother to make on the hind end of a chuck wagon," said Joseph Bailey (Cap) Warren. "Still, during cold weather I whip up a batch of chili about once every few weeks, and these new-style cowboys whine and blubber for it more often."

Cap Warren, a rangeland *cocinero* for more than fifty years, was once described by a rancher who was trying to lure him away from the Waggoner Ranch as "everything a chuck wagon cook ought to be, wrapped up in one snarling package."

When I knew him in the 1950s, Cap Warren was cooking on the almost ceaseless cattle roundups of the half-million-acre Waggoner Ranch, which sprawls over six counties in northwestern Texas near the Red River and has its head-quarters at Vernon.

1

Once when I was visiting with the Waggoner roundup crew I spent a whole day watching Cap Warren at his routine. The old boy became sort of bored with my presence and asked at the end of the day: "What you bird-dogging me fer?"

That morning, in early spring, Cap Warren arose from his bedroll at the usual time, four o'clock. As usual, he was in a bad humor, and for the usual reason. Mr. Warren had a low opinion of modern cowboys in general and the Waggoner Ranch punchers in particular, and the crew he was cooking for often had to listen to ill-tempered comment.

He was a tall man with the same athletic, 170-pound frame he'd had fifty years before when he quit cowboying to boss the chuck wagon. He hadn't had a haircut since spring roundup had started, and his thick white hair came down to a kind of duckbill in the back, giving him something of the look of an eighteenth-century gentleman with a powdered wig.

His "hood" (pronounced to rhyme with "rude"), or cook's assistant, was absent that morning. Normally, the hood would build the cook fires. By lantern light, Cap ignited mesquite chunks in a square iron stove. He ignored me until I asked him how present-day cowhands compared with those he'd known in the old days. He surveyed the Waggoner Ranch riders, asleep in their bedrolls under the tent which also protected the chuck wagon and the portable stove. And he said:

"Cowboys today is mostly a crowd of sissies. In the olden days we could have made camp here with nothing but a wagon and four mules, and my Dutch oven and my frying pans and stewers in a cowhide sling under the rear axle, and fetching the bedrolls in the wagon. Then they et what I gave them and got wet when it rained.

"Now look at this danged camp with this big truck for a chuck wagon, and tons of other machinery, and this here big tent for them hands to sleep under. This don't seem like a cow camp to me. With that tent and all, it seems like we're holding a gospel camp meeting."

The Waggoner Ranch, often called the Three D because that is the cattle brand, has twenty-one divisions, each with a line camp. That morning forty-seven cowboys were to gather cow creatures on a division called the Harts. The tent was pitched on a little rise near a windmill and line camp, actually a dwelling occupied by the line rider's family.

The morning was tolerably windy with promise of a dust storm by midmorning. Off in the lifting darkness were the restless whistling and stamping sounds of the 325-horse remuda being brought in by the wrangler.

"Ain't many left that would make a wart on the hind cheek of a real cowpuncher," continued Cap. "Now, fellow, you stay here and don't slow-trail me. I'll be back in a few minutes." He picked up the lantern and a big butcher knife, and went off to a storage house near the line camp. He came back with a load of steaks, each about two and a half inches thick, which he's sliced from a freshly killed beef. He had to make another trip before he had enough steaks for breakfast. Cap broiled or fried steaks for every meal after a beef had been butchered on the range.

"If I was cooking for real cowboys, I wouldn't have nothing but beef and bread and coffee this morning. Not with this bunch here, though. They got to have their fruit juices when they get up. And they got the gall to tell the cook how they want their eggs did."

Cap went to work making sourdough biscuits. He baked two big pans of biscuits before each meal. He made them in almost magician-like swiftness.

The Waggoner Ranch has a helicopter for many chores and errands. One of the plane's jobs was to fly over heavy brush and scare wild cattle into the open. This business of herding cattle with a helicopter came to the attention of a national television program and it sent some cameramen to the spring roundup that week. The day before, when Cap was making biscuits, he said one of the cameramen had asked him to pose over his dough with a rolling pin.

"I told that fuddy-grafter I didn't have no more use for a rolling pin than a hog has for a buggy whip. I roll out my biscuits by hand and choke them off into shape in the old style. Just like my mama taught me sixty-odd years ago."

The red truck chuck wagon had many steel compartments in the back of the bed, like those in a modern kitchen. The ingate doors dropped down to make a worktable. Cap could drive a truck, yet had such nostalgia for the old mule-drawn chuck wagons that he refused to be the truck's chauffeur and one of the young cowboys had to move it for him.

In one of the steel compartments he had a crock of yeast at work, the "starter" for his sourdough biscuits. Even when he joked, Cap's unwavering pale blue eyes kept serious. He said: "I got two young bullfrogs in that crock to keep my biscuit yeasts all worked up. Used to have an old bullfrog. But he got tired."

He put on an apron made of two flour sacks before he started broiling the steaks. The iron stove glowed red and took the chill off the air. When the biscuits and the steaks were almost ready, and coffee was boiling in a black pot, the cowboys began waking up, aroused by both the lovely smells and by Cap's whining, complaining baritone.

Cap prided himself on his biscuits, even more than on his proudest entree, son-of-a-bitch stew. He said it was his talent for biscuit making that shoved him, reluctantly he claimed, into a range cook's job back in 1912.

"Before that I was a cowboy and a danged good one. Everyone in that 1912 camp was tired of the old cook's biscuits. Ever' now and again we would find a cigarette butt in a biscuit. And them things baked out so heavy you could have took and th'owed one for over a hundred yards.

"Well it was knowed in camp that Mama had made me a pretty fair hand at baking. A passel of the boys teased me one morning to make up a couple of pans of biscuits. I done it.

"After that the wagon boss put the old cook back to driving a team. And I haven't been able to get shed of this cooking job since."

By this time, the Three D cowboys were ready for breakfast. Cap cooked eggs to order, although with a good deal of blasphemy. The riders served themselves. They scraped their plates clean and stacked them in a washtub when they were through.

Just before big daylight there was a drone in the sky over the cow camp. The helicopter was coming from Zacawiesta, the main ranch headquarters, about thirty miles away. The flying machine made an easy landing on a grassy pitch near the tent. The copter's rotors made slap-slap sounds and sent the 325-horse remuda into a state of noisy excitement.

Arriving in the plane were the ranch pilot and foreman Tony Hazlewood, a grim-faced old cowboy who had worked for the Three D since 1913. Hazlewood had fallen in love with the helicopter. From its upholstered throne, he could check on all of the ranch's half million acres in a few days. He could swiftly inspect the 2,500 miles of barbed wire fence and the 500 water holes, including three large artificial lakes.

In chasing wild cattle from mesquite jungles, the plane could do the work of twenty-five to thirty mounted men, wagon boss G. L. Proctor said. The machine would hover over the rumps of the beasts and frighten them out of the brush, sometimes literally driving the stock to the pens.

Cap Warren, no admirer of the helicopter, said: "If this keeps up, everyone of these sockwads on this roundup is going to want to cowboy in the air, and I'll be cooking for a crowd of mechanics. They is a lot of things, I'll have to own up, that that airyplane can do, only I wouldn't want to rope nothing from it."

The pilot and the foreman were drinking Cap's powerful boiled coffee when the old cook was in the midst of some angry complaints about how the riders were leaving their "gear and plunder" scattered around the chuck wagon.

"Cowboys now got way too much tackle, anyhow," he said. "In the olden day, a puncher usually had him just one bridle, one hackamore, and one saddle. Now it takes a chip wagon to tote all the spare bridles and hackamores these fellows need. And they scatter their gear and plunder over three acres."

It was saddling-up time. Red dust blew out of eroded gullies to the west of the camp. The punchers stood in a circle around the remuda and roped the horses of their choice in a red dirt fog, and then they saddled quickly and headed for the river bottoms to the west where there were wild horned cattle that had eluded a previous roundup.

Cap had the dishes boiling in the washtub (normally the hood would have done this chore) and he smoked his pipe and watched the saddling-up with some distaste.

"Horses ain't as wild as they used to be. I ain't seen one of them fellows th'owed in a week or more."

Mostly, the Three D cowboys listened to Cap's uncomplimentary talk without comment. A sixty-eight-year-old puncher named Harve Brothers put it this way: "Cap is a mighty fine cook. He can bullyrag me all he wants as long as he turns out wonderful biscuits, chili, and S.O.B. stew, and all the rest."

Now, though, listening to Cap carry on about the deplorable tameness of the current crop of horses in the remuda, Harve couldn't resist saying: "They is plenty of raunchy ponies in that remuda, Cap. Any time you want to do some cowboying, we got lots of horses that needs to be rode."

Bull Franklin, one of the ranch's four horse-breaking specialists, joined in the discussion: "Did you ever think, Cap, that we are doing a better job of making those old ponies polite than the horse-breakers did in your day? We usually have them acting pretty nice before the boys fall heir to them for the roundups."

This was in mid-April, and since February 4, Bull Franklin and the others had been breaking horses for the roundup.

"If you're spoiling to see folks th'owed, Cap, come down to the horse-breaking ranch when we're just starting to educate the young ponies," said another of the horse breakers, Justin

McCloskey.

Each of the cowboys had some broncs, or fresh graduates of the horse-breaking ranch, in his string for the roundup. Robert McElroy, a veteran hand, had, for example, a string of twelve "old horses" and five broncs.

McElroy, who had lived all his life on the Waggoner Ranch, came in for some left-handed praise from the cook during breakfast that morning: "You're a fair-to-middlin' cowboy, McElroy, but you ain't near the man your pappy was. Now there was a cowhand!"

McElroy explained to me that his father, the late Shinnery McElroy, had worked for the ranch from 1876 until his retirement in 1933.

"Paw strayed," said Robert McElroy. He wasn't speaking of his sire's morals; he meant that his father's main job had been searching for stray cattle wearing the Three D brand.

"Paw was sure good at working out the heavy brush country for cattle, and that's why they called him Shinnery. Before that hellycopter came along, I would have rated Paw the best at getting the old steers with the mossy horns out of the shinnery. He strayed way up in Indian Territory for the Three D in the olden days."

At breakfast, helping himself to some stewed fruit, McElroy spilled a little on the ground by the chuck wagon's ingate. Cap roared: "You people is just like a crowd of hogs. You can't lift nothing. You got to slop it out."

He continued to grumble until all the cowboys were gone on the morning's ride.

Despite the dirt and wind, spring showed on the land. The faces of the Hereford calves were incredibly white. Down in the river bottoms the flowering mesquite trees, with their pale green spring feathers, made shadows over the red earth.

Big stock trucks bounced over the dirt roads of the ranch, carrying cargoes of horses and cowboys. Instead of making long horseback rides over the half million acres, the men and their mounts often hitched rides on the trucks, with foreman

Hazlewood broadcasting orders by radio from the helicopter and with the motor vehicles monitoring his commands.

Harve Brothers, still a first-rate cowboy at sixty-eight, had a busy morning. He roped wild cows with grotesquely swollen udders, threw and tied them, milked them, and doctored the stoppages which caused the udders to swell. He pulled a steer from a bog in the bottoms. With thorns pricking at his leather chaps, he rode hard through the brush. The dust was thick and settled on his face until he looked as if he were blacked up for a minstrel show when he got back to the chuck wagon a little before the rest of the hands.

The old cowboy and his weary horse (he would change to a fresh mount after the noon meal) returned to the chuck wagon before the others because he happened to hitch a ride in a stock truck that was going to the loading pens. Then he rode in a station wagon to the cow camp with one of the ranch's owners who just happened to be at the loading pens.

Cap saw Harve coming up in the station wagon.

"You're sure getting soft, Mr. Brothers," said the cook. "Pretty soon you'll be asking for your own hellycopter."

Harve made no reply except to ask if the iced tea was ready yet.

"Hear that," Cap told me. "In the old day, I didn't serve nothing but coffee and water on a roundup. Now they want iced tea when it's hot and hot chocolate if they is a norther. And, you know, one of them young, so-called cowpunchers come creeping up to me the other day and wanted me to bake him some cookies!"

Cap didn't talk for a while after that. He was running a little behind on preparation of a noon meal for fifty men or more. He went to work on his second pan of sourdough biscuits with easy speed, rolling the dough by hand and chocking it off in the old style, just as his mama taught him to do sixty-odd years before.

1. The Original, Texas-Style "Bowl of Red"

"Congress should pass a law making it mandatory for all restaurants serving chili to follow a Texas recipe."

Harry James

This isn't a cookbook, although some recipes will be recited. This is about the lore of chili con carne and some less known native foods of the Southwest, such as son-of-a-bitch stew, made from the cheapest and most vitamin-packed cuts of beef.

This book will tell the stories of some cooks who operated in the true tradition, the way Cap Warren did.

They never worked in inspiring surroundings. Just in hole-in-the-wall chili parlors or at the hind end of a chuck wagon parked in the dusty wilderness. And yet they were geniuses in their fashion. The sad thing is that, while the memory of their produce and even their personalities live on, some of their names are lost to recollection.

The book will also tell the story of the "chili wars," the great annual Terlingua, Texas, chili cookoffs that grew from

9

a tongue-in-cheek local promotion into practically an international sport.

When speaking of a bowl of red, I refer to chili con carne — honest-to-God chili, and not the dreadful stuff masquerading as chili which is served in nine out of ten cafés. Real chili con carne is a haunting, mystic thing. As Margaret Cousins, my former Doubleday editor, once wrote to me: "Chili is not so much a food as a state of mind. Addictions to it are formed early in life and the victims never recover. On blue days in October I get this passionate yearning for a bowl of chili, and I nearly lose my mind, for there is nowhere I can go in New York City to buy the real thing ..."

Mrs. Lyndon B. Johnson experienced the same autumnal "chili pangs" — only in November. The former First Lady wrote me: "As for a quotation for your book, my feeling about chili is this — along in November, when the first norther strikes, and the skies are gray, along about five o'clock in the afternoon, I get to thinking how good chili would taste for supper.

"It always lives up to expectations. In fact, you don't even mind the cold November winds."

Harry James, the great horn player, declared: "Next to jazz music, there is nothing that lifts the spirit and strengthens the soul more than a good bowl of chili."

In cliché thinking, chili con carne is a Mexican food. This isn't true. The Mexicans disclaim authorship, as will be explained in the third chapter along with some theories of how chili con carne originated in the southwestern reaches of the United States.

The emphasis in this book will be on the world-famous, seldom-found-today, original, Texas-style bowl of red. I happen to be a fourth-generation Texan and so open to charges of chauvinism when I say that the best chili is now made in Texas, and has been made in this province since the dim beginnings of the piperine delight.

Almost all the real "chili heads" agree on the superiority of the original bowl of Texas-style red. I was on the receiving end of an international "chili poll" as the result of an article I wrote for *The Saturday Evening Post* titled, "That Bowl of Fire Called Chili." This short article on the history of chili, containing two recipes, resulted in my receiving more than 29,000 friendly letters from all over the free world. For several weeks after the *Post* article appeared it looked as if the post office had just blown up on my desk. The mail is still coming in. The majority of the letters — or rather, the ones I've had time to read — expressed nostalgia over experience with Texas-style chili, and the desire to experience it again.

Hank Richards of Burbank, California, wrote that his taste buds actually ache with longing when he recalls the chili of his boyhood, at Texas Jack's Place in Springfield, Illinois.

Jim Valentine of Dallas said that he is almost overcome with emotion when he thinks of a chili parlor he patronized years ago at Wills Point, Texas. Mr. Valentine described the operator of the chili parlor as a "Da Vinci of the pepper pods who believed that every pot of chili had a soul. He stood guard during the long hours of conception . . ."

Harry James said that during the years he traveled over the country with his jazz band he was constantly on a search of cafés that served Texas-style chili. He said he seldom found one.

"Congress should pass a law making it mandatory for all restaurants serving chili to follow a Texas recipe," suggested Mr. James.

Lyndon B. Johnson, thirty-sixth President of the United States, certainly tried to avoid the image of a Texas braggart. Still, friends have heard the former President say: "Chili concocted outside of Texas is usually a weak, apologetic imitation of the real thing. One of the first things I do when I get home to Texas is to have a bowl of red. There is simply nothing better."

Real chili aficionados may quarrel with Mr. Johnson's recipe, which leaves one of the ingredients out — beef suet

— and puts two other ingredients in — tomatoes and onions. President Johnson's favorite is styled "Pedernales River chili," as prepared on the LBJ Ranch on the Pedernales (pronounced "purr-DIN-alice") River in the Texas hill country by his famous cook, Mrs. Zephyr Wright.

As for the omitted beef suet, this ingredient was left out of the recipe after President Johnson had a severe heart attack when he was majority leader of the United States Senate. The LBJ formula also calls for venison, if available. The meat of the hill country deer is usually very lean. Otherwise beef, as fat-free as possible, is used.

The ingredients for Pedernales River chili are: 4 pounds of chili-meat; 1 large chopped onion; 2 cloves of garlic; 1 teaspoon of orégano (Spanish for the wild marjoram, which grows in Texas); 1 teaspoon of ground cumin seeds; 6 teaspoons of chili powder (or more if you want it warmly flavored); 2 sixteen-ounce cans of tomatoes; salt to suit you; 2 cups of hot water. Put the meat, the onion, and the garlic cloves, which have been finely chopped, in a large skillet and sear until grayish. Add the rest of the ingredients, bring to a boil, lower the heat, and simmer for an hour with the cover on the skillet. Skim off the grease. Serves 12.

In her letter, Mrs. Johnson said: "I am well aware of the article on chili con carne you wrote for *The Saturday Evening Post* because we still get letters concerning it. Pedernales River chili is an old recipe, with the name coined out of public necessity. So many requests came in for the recipe, and I wanted to send out something typical of Texas and a favorite of my husband's. It was easier to give the recipe a name, have it printed on a card and make it available.

"It has been almost as popular as the government pamphlet on the care and feeding of children."

The original Texas-style chili didn't contain any vegetables except chili peppers, the burning capsicums, a few other spices derived from the plant kingdom — no tomatoes or chopped onion as in the Pedernales River recipe.

The "original" was simply bite-size or coarsely ground (half-inch-diameter plate holes is the grinder setting recommended) beef or other mature meats (never, never veal) cooked slowly and for a long time in boon companionship with the pulp of chili peppers, crushed powder from the curly leaves of orégano, ground cumin seeds (*comino* in Spanish and sometimes so labeled), and chopped garlic cloves.

The first and worst chore of chili making, according to the original formula, is preparing the peppers — in the next chapter there will be a recitation on the history and nature of these passionate vegetables. Ask for sun-dried *anchos* or a similar type developed by the Japanese, styled "Jap peppers." You'll be surprised how easy it is to get these peppers in stores, especially if you live in the western or southern reaches of the nation. In most big cities, too, there are Mexican food stores.

For chili with a very "elevated" flavor use four pepper pods for each pound of beef. For mild chili try half as many pods. If you can't get the pepper pods, chili powder will do handsomely, although it doesn't impart the same delicate sting as the pepper pods. A heaping tablespoon of chili powder has about the same "power rating" as one average-size chili pepper.

If possible, pick pods of a reddish hue to give the chili its approved coloration. Still, those capsicums may be yellowish, greenish, purplish in maturity and still have the same wild personality as the red ones. If you can't get red, mix in one level tablespoon of paprika when the pods have been reduced to pulp. The paprika will make the mixture more rosy and won't affect the taste.

Wash the peppers and remove the stems and seeds. (Don't touch your eyes during this operation and wash your hands thoroughly afterward.) Boil the pods in a little water for thirty minutes, or until the skins can be removed easily. Then grind, chop, or run through a colander the now skinless, seedless, stemless pods. Save the peppery water in which the pods were boiled. Use it for cooking the chili and for adding water if necessary. Be as conservative as possible on the water unless you want the chili to be soupy.

For this "original" recipe, three pounds of lean beef is the main vehicle. Stewing meat is excellent if it's fat-free, but never, never use prime beef, for it will turn into mush. The old directions call for an eighth of a pound of rendered beef kidney suet. For this recipe we will make it optional. If you like greasy chili and are under no diet inhibitions, go ahead with the suet. It does add flavor, and the grease can be skimmed off in the final stages of cooking.

Just as in the Pedernales River recipe, sear the three pounds of beef until it is gray in color. Perhaps you will need a little cooking oil on the face of the skillet for this operation. A big iron skillet, holding at least four quarts, can be used for the whole process except the searing. Or else you can have ready a pot, preferably an iron one. Into this pot (or the skillet) drop the beef, the optional rendered suet, the pepper pods, and as much of the peppery liquid as you think you'll need to keep the meat from burning. About two inches of water rising above the beef is usually right. Bring this to a boil and then turn down the heat and simmer for thirty minutes.

Take the pot (or skillet) off the stove. Add 1 level teaspoon of orégano powder (or the curly leaves of orégano), 1 level tablespoon of crushed cumin seeds, 1 level tablespoon of salt, 1 level tablespoon of powdered cayenne pepper, 1 tablespoon of Tabasco sauce, and chopped garlic pods to suit your taste, but at least 2. If you want to be adventurous and to add more red color — although this wasn't in the original — pour in 3 level tablespoons of chili powder.

Put the mixture back on the stove and bring it to a boil again, lower the heat, and simmer for 45 minutes, keeping the lid on as much as possible. Stir when necessary, but too much stirring will tear up the meat, especially if the meat is too tender. Add the peppered water only if you think the mixture will burn otherwise.

Take the pot off the stove again. Most contemporary chili makers skim off the grease. The old-timers didn't, or not all of the grease, anyway. It's up to you. Personally, I'm antigrease.

Optional is 2 tablespoons of Masa Harina. This is Mexican corn meal, made in the ancient Indian way, for tortillas and tamales. You can get instant Masa Harina now in most stores. Instant Masa Harina was developed by Quaker Oats under a commission from the Mexican Government to save its people from making the stuff in the old and arduous Indian way. Masa Harina will not only add a subtle, tamale-like taste, but it will thicken or "tighten" the chili. If Masa Harina isn't available, settle for ordinary corn meal or wheat flour.

Cook, actually simmer most of the way, for another thirty minutes, or until the meat is done. During this last thirty minutes, do a lot of tasting to see if the seasoning suits you. If it's not peppery enough — although it certainly should be for most folks — toss in three more chili pods. These final pods have the seeds, stems, and skins removed but are not chopped up.

If you're making chili for the first time or if you're a tender-mouthed type, you'd better start off with the mild, two-pods-to-a-pound version on the peppers and don't get reckless and throw in those three whole pods during the last thirty minutes of cooking.

As mentioned before, the olden chili makers had a horror of putting tomatoes and onions into chili. They figured these additions would convert their beloved meat entree into a stew. Still, Wick Fowler of Austin, Texas, one of the best contemporary chili cooks, puts fifteen ounces of tomato sauce in a recipe calling for three pounds of beef. Mr. Fowler figures that the tomato sauce adds color and thickening and the flavor of it is lost amid the powerful spices. Wick never uses suet, and he is one of those who seldom serve chili on the day of its conception. He keeps it in the refrigerator overnight to "seal in the spices." Also, more grease will rise to the top during the stay in the icebox and can be skimmed off before you reheat the chili.

Before World War II, the Lang family operated two memorable chili parlors in Dallas. Decades after the establishments closed, old-timers speak reverently, lovingly, of "Lang's chili."

Actually, each parlor had its own version of chili con carne. At each parlor, formula "secrets" were guarded jealously. The most obvious difference was that at one Lang's the chili meat was cut into cubes while at the other it was coarsely ground.

Both Langses certainly had a good "security system" going, even after the parlors had passed from the scene. For years I tried to get a real Lang recipe. Finally, Mrs. J. W. Simpson of Dallas obliged me with "the one which called for cubing the beef, the best recipe." Mrs. Simpson said she'd "kept quiet about my Lang chili recipe for many years. Yet now it's been so long since the parlors closed that I guess it's all right to print the recipe."

Her late husband, Jim Simpson, was a friend of one of the Lang cooks, Will Clark. After long persuasion, Will Clark wrote down the directions for Mr. Simpson. The principal *secret* seems to have been that the comino was parched and mashed.

"Will Clark mentioned no water in the directions," said Mrs. Simpson. "I do add a little water, although you'll be surprised how much juice results from the braising of the beef."

By doing some mathematical sums you can build a smaller chili pot, but here the ingredients will be given in the proportions used by Will Clark in that Lang's kitchen long ago:

"Sixteen pounds of lean (no fat), mature beef cut into cubes about the size of your thumb; 1½ pounds of lard or cooking oil; ½ cup of finely cut garlic; 1 saucer of flour or

Masa Harina; 1½ pounds of dried chili peppers, skinned, deseeded, and mashed, preferably mashed almost into a pulp; ½ cup of parched and mashed comino (don't burn the comino during the parching, Clark warned)."

As relayed from Mrs. Simpson, these are Will Clark's directions, which, incidentally, are much less time-consuming than is often the case for making real Texas-style chili.

"Get the lard or oil hot in a skillet — you'll need a big one — and then add the cubed meat and half of the garlic. You then braise the meat until it is brown and tender. You have an iron kettle for a chili pot, and it's a big one, on the stove. Pour the liquid from the beef into the chili pot. Then braise the meat some more in the skillet until the beef is dry and still browner. Sift in the flour and put the meat in the liquid in the chili pot and stir while it simmers for 30 minutes. Add the chili peppers and cook for another 15 minutes. Add the comino and the rest of the garlic and cook for 10 minutes. That's all."

Mrs. Simpson said that this makes highly seasoned chili. And she usually put in only about a fourth as many chili peppers as Will Clark's directions called for.

Along the upper Rio Grande in Texas and in New Mexico, chili verde con carne is quite popular. This is made with fresh green chili peppers, picked in the succulent stage but just before they mature.

The "original" chili recipe can be followed, using fresh green chili pods. The methods for skinning them are different, though. Snip the stem and the other end of the pod. Most chili verde cooks leave in the seeds. Put the fresh pepper pods on a mesh wire over an electric heating unit, turned up high. Flip over the chilies frequently so the outer skin will blister evenly. Or put the peppers on a foil-covered oven rack, about three inches below a high flame, also turning frequently for even blistering. Then plunge the pods into ice water. After this process the skins can be removed easily.

You start at the stem end and peel the outer skin downward. The pods are then pulped for adding to the chili con carne mixture.

Dr. Roy M. Nakayama, a plant scientist at New Mexico State University in Las Cruces, near El Paso, who specializes in research on hot chili peppers, usually makes his chili verde with a fresh green chili sauce, but without orégano, cumin seeds, or garlic. The result has a fresh, wild sting, but no real chili con carne buff would thoroughly approve of it.

To make this fresh green sauce, or 1½ cups of it, you need 8 to 12 fresh green pods, 1 medium-size ripe tomato, and ½ teaspoon of salt. When the chilies have been peeled, chop them very fine. Peel the tomato and then, with your hands, mash it until it, too, is in liquid-pulp form. Combine the chilies, the tomato, the salt, and stir well. This will keep for four or five days in a refrigerator, if covered.

Professor Nakayama's recipe calls for 1 pound of very lean beef, cut in 1-inch-diameter cubes, and cooked in a hot skillet, under low heat, until the meat is brown. Then add from 1¼ to 1½ cups of the fresh green chili sauce, ½ teaspoon of salt, ½ cup of chopped onions, ½ cup of tomatoes, and ½ cup of hot water. Bring to a boil and then simmer until the meat is done and tender.

2. "The Grains of Paradise"

"After them groweth the Cods, greene at first and when they be ripe of brave colour, glittering like red corrall, and of a hot, biting taste."

John Gerard on chili peppers
in a 1597 botanical paper

In Mexico and in the back country of the Southwestern United States, hot chili pepper-worshiping folks call the fire-veined pod *malagueta* or *amomo,* both of which mean "grain of paradise."

In Texas and in New Mexico along the Rio Grande, malagueta and amomo refer to wild little round peppers, also called chilipiquines, piquines, or tepins. Because they grow wild, chilipiquines were usually used in the olden days for making chili con carne. The large chilies — ancho (wide) is an example — are perennials in the tropics but are annuals and require cultivation in the Southwest.

Today, chilipiquines are seldom used for adding pungency and flavor (these are different qualities in a chili pepper) to chili con carne, but on ranches piquines are still in much demand for seasoning the meat filling of tamales.

Now, most chili con carne is made from chili peppers with larger and longer pods, such as the ancho of Mexico or the California long red (Anaheim), or "Jap peppers," carefully cultivated on plantations in California, Mexico, Japan, New Mexico, and Texas.

Columbus's discovery of America also led to the discovery of chili con carne — or rather the ingredient the world needed to make it, chili peppers. For convenience these are called red peppers, although they mature in other colors. They are the fruits of the capsicum, a sometimes bland but more often bitingly pungent plant of a family which includes the potato and the tomato. *Not* in the same family are the plants which produce the berries for the pepper of antiquity, *Piper nigrum,* from which is made black or white powdered pepper.

"Chilli" is the Nahuatl, or Aztec, word for the plant. In 1493, Peter Martyr wrote that Columbus brought home with him "peppers more pungent than that from the Caucus."

In the time of Columbus, pepper was a commodity as valuable as gold. Although the burning capsicums are now grown over much of the world, they were native to tropical, continental America and the West Indies. In his book *Economic Botany,* Dr. Albert F. Hill calls the red peppers "America's most important contribution to the spices." So important were they considered that the country of Chile was named for the burning capsicum.

By 1600, chili peppers were being cultivated around the globe. Africa raised the hottest (although not the most flavorful), such as the *gandar* and the *mambasa.* Japan developed its own strains of hot peppers, and "Jap peppers," especially two varieties called *hontaca* and *santaka,* are much in demand for chili con carne and other culinary purposes.

The first scientific treatise on the burning capsicums I have found appeared in a 1597 book, *The Herball, or Generall Historie of Plantes,* by John Gerard of England. The British botanist, in his description of "long-codded" and "shortcodded" chilies, seemed to be referring to peppers similar to the ancho and its smaller, rounder, hotter cousin called *ensensada* in Mexico.

"The flowers groweth along the stalks out of the wings of the leaves," wrote John Gerard. "After them groweth the Cods, greene at first and when they be ripe of a brave colour, glittering like red corall, and of a hot, biting taste . . ."

Gerard had trouble growing the plants in his English garden, and had to put them in pots and bring them indoors during the cold months. He gave the chilies a rather mixed review. First he quoted another botanist: "Auicen writeth that the Ginny [Guinea] peppers killeth dogs." Then Gerard reported from his own consumption of them that the peppers stirred up the gastric juices, "warmeth the stomacke and helpeth greatly the digestion of meates.

"These plantes are brought from forren countries, such as Ginny [Guinea] in the Indies [America] and those parts, into Spain and Italy, from whence we received seedes for our English garden, where they come to fruite bearing but the cod doth not come to the bright red colour which by nature it doth posses, which happened by reason of these unkindly yeares that are past, but we expect better when God shall send us a hot and temperate yeare.

"The seedes hereof must be sowen in a bed of hot horse dung, as muske melons are, and removed into pots when the plantes hath gotten three or four leaves that they may be more conveniently carried from place to place to receive the heate of the sunne, and towards autumne to be carried into the house to avoide the injuries of colde nights at the time of the yeare when they are to beare the fruite.

"Ginny peppers are extreme hot, even in the fourth degree, that is to say farre hotter and drier than Auicen showeth dog ginger to be. Ginny peppers hath the taste of pepper [black powdered pepper] but not the power or vertue, notwithstanding that in Spain and in sundrie parts of the Indies they do use them to dresse their meates therewith, as we do with calectue [Calcutta?] pepper, but Ginnies hath in them a more malicious qualitie."

Dr. Roy Nakayama, the New Mexico State University horticulturist, says that the most confusing thing nowadays about chili peppers is the nomenclature for all the varieties.

"The terminology for chilies in this country and in Mexico is often completely different," said Dr. Nakayama, a New Mexico native of Japanese ancestry who is in charge of experimental breeding of 1,500 acres of chili peppers near Las Cruces on the Rio Grande.

The chilies have long been products of prime importance in New Mexico and in the adjacent El Paso area, according to Ruth W. Sneed, a food specialist at New Mexico State University. For instance, she quoted an 1863 New Mexico newspaper that the United States had spent fifty thousand dollars that year for improving the roads "for intercommunication and the transportation of chilies colorado to market."

The native chilies grown in New Mexico were variable and of a poor grade, said Ruth Sneed. New Mexico State's scientific research on chilies, according to a booklet Ruth Sneed wrote on the pepper, "started back in 1907 when Fabian Garcia selected and planted the seeds of three varieties of chilies. The search was for a better chili for New Mexico. The goal has remained clear and distinct — larger, smoother, thick-meated, shoulderless pods. Dr. Garcia, then horticulturist and later director of the University's agricultural experiment station, started out with chili colorado, chili negro, and chili pasilla."

Dr. Garcia developed chilies of various pungencies or heat contents, suitable for the various soils and climates of New Mexico. As Ruth Sneed wrote in the booklet: "The new varieties didn't just happen, but were the result of careful planning and selection. For instance, there's Rio Grande, medium in pungency and a popular variety when grown in the Hatch, New Mexico, area but a mild green chili when produced around Albuquerque. Sandia A and B were carefully selected for their esters or oils to give the flavor and pungency the people of Bernalillo and Sandoval counties prefer. Sandia A develops early, has a shorter pod and a high degree of pungency. Sandia B has a flavor very similar to unimproved native chili."

Not everyone knows it, but chili peppers are a rich source of Vitamins A and C. Vitamin A is indicated by the carotenoid (yellow and red pigments) content of the brilliantly colored peppers. This is retained even after the chilies are canned or dried, although to a lesser degree when dried or powdered. The ascorbic acid or Vitamin C increases in a chili as it matures. About two thirds of the ascorbic acid remains in canned or frozen chilies, but Vitamin C is adversely affected by heat and oxidation, and is lost when the chilies are dried.

The heat or pungency of chilies is never lost, but the flavor can change. When a chili pepper loses some of its carotenoid pigment, some of the flavor is lost. High flavor and high color go together. So when you're picking the chilies to make a bowl of red, try to get those in which the pigments haven't been destroyed by heat or long storage.

Another New Mexico scientist has been doing a different kind of research on chili peppers. She is Dr. Lora M. Shields, chairman of the biology department at Highlands University in Las Vegas, New Mexico. Years ago she noted the low incidence of heart diseases among Spanish-Americans and Indians in the Southwest. These were people who eat a lot of chili peppers.

Dr. Shields emphasizes that her work in this field is in the preliminary stage. Yet she has found that these people, especially those who cling to ancient gastronomic practices, reach the peak of lipids or fatty substances in their bloodstream at thirty to thirty-nine years of age, and then there is a decrease. In contrast, "Anglos" of the Southwest who live on typical American diets may not reach the lipid peak until age sixty-nine.

Lora Shields, a native of New Mexico, has specialized her study of dietary habits and their effect on heart diseases on the triglycerides, elements or building stones of cholesterol, the fatty substance in the bloodstream strongly suspected by many medical doctors of contributing to coronary diseases.

Dr. Shields, who, with a colleague, "scooped" the scientific world in research on the effects of radiation on desert plants, hopes to give more validity to her "chili pepper theory" with a test group of healthy New Mexico penitentiary inmates of various ages. These men have volunteered to subsist for a long period of time on nothing but native foods, with the emphasis on chili peppers. This should make for a happy group of felons, and some "chili heads" in other state penitentiaries will probably want to become Lora Shields's guinea pigs.

Dr. Shields said in a Highlands University publication that "the action of chili peppers consumed often and liberally may rid the body of enough fats to lower the consumer's blood fat level and reduce his chances of having a heart attack."

She quotes state statistics which indicate that 40 percent more Latins and Indians, on their native diets, live beyond the age of seventy than do the Anglos.

Early-day folks in the Southwest ascribed wonderful things to the "grains of paradise." For sample, Ab Blocker, one of the most memorable of the cattle drivers from Texas to Kansas, claimed that chilipiquines would cure the rabies.

Malagueta or amomo figured in a delightful fiction story written by the late James Street in a 1955 issue of *The Saturday Evening Post.* The yarn is about a chili pepper-eating contest in a village in the state of Tabasco, Mexico.

This fictional village had an inhabitant, an Indian called Hilario, who had been undefeated for many years as the local champion consumer of fiery peppers. An "Americano," a plant scientist, one Hoyle, came to town and established a reputation for his tolerance of the most pungent chilies.

He was quickly recruited by the jealous "Ladinos," those

of Spanish blood, to engage the Indian, Hilario, in a pepper-eating contest. There was much betting between the Ladinos and those of pure Indian ancestry on the outcome.

The rules were that champion and contender could take either a sip of beer or a nibble of tortilla one minute after eating each pepper. Sweating visibly or "breathing hard" meant disqualification and defeat.

So they gobbled a series of hot-tempered peppers which Mr. Street described as red frenzies, green terrors, yellow furies, green infernos, etc. Pods of malagueta, the grains of paradise, evidently chilipiquines, were the final and supreme test. Mr. Street told of Hoyle's reaction to the first bites of malagueta: "The heat jolted me. The roof of my mouth corroded, and the tissues of my cheeks contracted like cellophane."

Hoyle was sure that he had Hilario beaten after they downed the grains of paradise. The Indian was obviously near collapse. Yet the kindly American became overcome with pity for the poor Indians, who had wagered all their possessions on their champion. Hoyle disqualified himself by reaching for a bite of tortilla before the time limit.

My friend Jim Street died shortly before the publication of this story. But if by malagueta he meant chilipiquines, then almost any cowhand in southwestern Texas could have whipped Mr. Street's fictional pepper-eating heroes. Down where these little chilies grow wild, the cowboys eat them as if they were peanuts.

Piquines there begin to bear in May and are palatable until cold weather withers them. At first they are green in color, and gradually become cherry red, in most cases, although some mature a bright yellow. The green ones are juicier and milder than the mature ones, although this is a relative thing. For even the greenest are like fire.

I have been a guest at the great King Ranch near Corpus Christi when the peppers are in season, and a branch of fresh chilipiquines is placed by your plate at mealtime. Or, if the grains of paradise aren't in the bearing stage, you get a small plate of dried or preserved ones.

Out on the rangelands, cowpunchers or sheepherders carry piquines in their pockets, in case the cook is out of them. The berries are mashed up in pinto beans or eaten with casually flavored meat.

Major Tom Armstrong of the Armstrong Ranch, near Armstrong, Texas, bordering the King Ranch, is typical of cattlemen who take along several pocket boxes of chilipiquines when they travel. It must create quite a stir among the waiters in continental restaurants when these cowmen take out their little cases of the grains of paradise to spice up the cuisine.

Wolves, coyotes, and other wild creatures relish piquines. There is a saying among the range people when the peppers come in season: "We must hurry and beat the birds to the chilies." For birds, especially wild turkeys and mockingbirds, have a passion for the burning capsicum.

"Wild turkeys make pigs out of themselves during piquines season. And it flavors their meat. There's no better turkey than a chili-pepper-fed one," says Alex Garcia, who makes the celebrated chili con carne at Otto Zernermann's City Market in Kingsville, headquarters town for the King Ranch. Alex is fairly typical of contemporary chili cooks, for he uses anchos for chili con carne but turns to chilipiquines when he can get them for the meat filling of tamales.

3. Chili History and Legend

"Wish I had time for just one more bowl of chili."
Alleged dying words
of Kit Carson

One contemporary Mexican dictionary has this scornful definition of chili con carne: "A detestable dish sold from Texas to New York City and erroneously described as Mexican." The editor of that dictionary must have, at some time, made a journey to New York by way of Texas and run into some very bad café chili en route.

The late E. DeGolyer, first a scholar and secondly a Dallas multimillionaire, spent some of his younger days in Mexico as an oil operator. Mr. DeGolyer said that chili should be called "chili à la Americano" because the term chili is generic in Mexico and defines no special dish. In Mexico it simply means a hot pepper.

DeGolyer believed that chili con carne began as the "pemmican of the Southwest" in the late 1840s. He found records that Texans pounded together dried beef, beef fat, dried chili peppers (in most cases chilipiquines), and salt into a kind of pemmican before making wilderness journeys to the

California gold fields. This amounted to brick chili, only much more concentrated than brick chili today. It could be boiled in pots on the trail.

Mr. DeGolyer's "chili pemmican" certainly wasn't widely popular by the 1860s, however. I've searched diligently and haven't found a reference to chili con carne in any letters or reports of Texas soldiers in the Civil War.

In the early 1950s, Texas had more surviving soldiers of the 1861-65 war than all the other states combined. There were six of them, all ex-Confederates. In addition, I found a blue-eyed Latin, a native of Brownsville, aged an authenticated 116, who had been adjudged physically unfit for service in the Confederate Army, which must have made him the world's oldest 4-F.

All seven of these ancients had lived in Texas since before the War Between the States. All except one, the blue-eyed Latin, were lovers of chili con carne. All agreed that their first experience with chili was in small cafés or from sidewalk vendors in San Antonio in the 1880s. Two of them mentioned that by 1890 it was a Southwest custom "to go to town on Saturday night and have a bowl or two of chili."

The only report I've read of a Civil War veteran eating chili before the 1880s appeared in a not-very-reliable California periodical. This paper claimed that the dying words in 1868 of Christopher (Kit) Carson, the great frontiersman, mountain man, and Union Army regimental commander in New Mexico, were: "Wish I had time for just one more bowl of chili." Kit Carson had done some prowling in Texas along the Rio Grande before the Civil War and may have sampled some early chili con carne down that way. Two of his most reliable biographers, though, don't mention chili con carne as one of old Kit's favorites, and record that his dying words were: *"Adios, compadres! Adios,* doctor," his way of phrasing it suggesting that he didn't include his medical man among his friends.

There is much evidence that chili con carne had its beginnings in Texas, possibly in San Antonio, in the early nineteenth century. Only it wasn't much known outside of poor folks' kitchens until the 1880s.

Two San Antonio writers, Maury Maverick, Jr. and Charles Ramsdell, frequently advance the argument that chili con carne originated in their home town, and they do it convincingly. Ramsdell, who spends much time in Mexico, wrote in his *San Antonio: An Historical and Pictorial Guide* (the best San Antonio guidebook published): "Chili, as we know it in the United States, cannot be found in Mexico today except in a few spots which cater to tourists. If chili had come from Mexico, it would still be there. For Mexicans, especially those of Indian ancestry, do not change their culinary customs from one generation, or even from one century, to another."

Ramsdell believes that chili con carne originated in San Antonio "among the poorest classes of people" by the third decade of the nineteenth century. J. C. Clopper is one of Ramsdell's witnesses, perhaps his best one. Clopper, who came from Cincinnati, Ohio, and settled on Clopper's Point in San Jacinto Bay near present-day Houston, may have been the first to write about chili, at least in its beginnings.

He wrote of a visit to San Antonio in 1828: "When they [poor families in San Antonio] have to pay for their meat in market, a very little is made to suffice for a family; it is generally cut into a kind of hash with nearly as many peppers as there are pieces of meat — this is all stewed together."

In searching for mentions of chili, I read a half-dozen articles on San Antonio published in the 1870s, most of them pretty hard going but one a really charming thing in an 1877 issue of *Harper's* magazine by one Harriet Prescott Spofford. In none of these articles, not even that of Harriet Spofford, evidently a very close observer, was there any reference to chili con carne or to the "chili queens," sidewalk vendors of chili who were to become such a conspicuous part of the night scene in San Antonio a little later.

Sidney Lanier, the poet, and also a good reporter, came to

San Antonio in the early 1870s to try and get over his consumption. He doesn't mention chili con carne or the chili queens.

Writers first begin to mention the chili queens in San Antonio around 1880. These picturesque vendors would appear around dusk in the downtown plazas, including Alamo Plaza. Carts carried their crude tables, pots, and other gear. The chili con carne was already cooked and in caldrons. Charcoal or mesquite fires were started to keep the chili simmering and sending forth its peppery perfumes on the night air. This was part of the sales pitch.

Usually there were checkerboard-patterned oilskins over the tables and, sometimes, stools for the customers. Each chili queen had a big, ornate lamp, often an antique, with globes of red, yellow, orange, or some other vivid color to catch the eyes of customers, who had already been hooked by the chili scent.

The chili queens dressed gaily and, according to one account, pinned bunches of roses, in season, "to their bosoms." Street musicians serenaded the chili eaters. The bright lamps of the queens, the smells of gently bubbling chili and wood smoke — these would have certainly inspired a poet such as Lanier if the queens had been in business when he was there.

William Sydney Porter, or O. Henry, the short-story master, was the first, it seems, to write about the chili queens in a fiction story. O. Henry came to Texas in 1882. As in the case of Sidney Lanier, he hoped the dry climate would improve his health. He worked on a ranch in La Salle County, southwest of San Antonio, and then he lived for a long time in Austin, which is eighty miles northeast of San Antonio.

It's a shame that O. Henry's "chili story" is probably one of the worst he ever wrote. It is called "The Enchanted Kiss" and the main character in the yarn is a shy drugstore clerk named Tansey: "Often Tansey strolled down to these stands [those of the chili queens] to partake of the delectable chili con carne, a dish evolved by the genius of Mexico, comprised of meats minced with aromatic herbs and the poignant chili colorado.

"The titillating odor of this concoction came now, on the breeze, to the nostrils of Tansey, awakening in him hunger for it . . ."

Actually, Tansey, the shy chili head, is having a hallucination. And one of the creatures of this hallucination is a former captain of the Spanish army that conquered Mexico in 1519. The captain has lived on and remained youthful for hundreds of years by eating chili con carne, made by the most loathsome methods.

"The Enchanted Kiss" shows that O. Henry believed chili con carne originated in Mexico. But then he never was much of a historical researcher.

The chili queens continued to reign by night on San Antonio streets until 1943. Then city health regulations forced them to conform with the same sanitary rules as restaurants. This was asking too much. The queens, with their caldrons and their bright lamps, were driven from the plazas.

How many communities in the Southwest gradually became aware of San Antonio chili con carne is illustrated in a story told by Roy F. Hall of McKinney, a large town just north of Dallas. According to Mr. Hall, an authority on McKinney's past, chili con carne was unknown there until 1890. Significantly, it was introduced by an old black fellow named Myers, Christian name lost to history, who had just returned from a trip to San Antonio. (Three years later, Chicago got its first taste of chili at the world's fair of that year when a "San Antonio Chilley Stand" went up on the grounds.)

Myers had a small café on the town square of McKinney. In 1890 he had already been renowned for two decades for his "special beef stew." It was said that Jesse and Frank James stopped off in McKinney several times, not to rob the bank but to eat Myers' wonderful stew.

Roy Hall was a child in 1890. Along with some adult relatives he was in Myers' café the night the old cook served his first pot made "from the chilley receipt I got down in Santone."

"I dearly loved my first bowl of red," said Mr. Hall, "although it was a hot enough with peppers to boil on a cold stove. Old Myers' chili started trouble in our town. Most folks relished the new dish. There were some, however, who maintained that it would ruin your insides. Heads of families forbade their children to eat the stuff. Of course, that just made the kids even more determined to sneak into Myers' place and sample it.

"The chili con carne dispute got so warm that it was taken up by the newspapers with editorials and letters to the editor. A few ministers preached sermons against indulgence in a food which they said was almost as hot as hell's brimstones. Soup of the Devil, one called it.

"In the meantime, though, Myers' chili was 'winning the war.' It was soon outselling his special beef stew. And the chili furor gradually died down."

Despite all this evidence that chili con carne was invented in the nineteenth century, probably in San Antonio, and almost certainly in Texas, there are those who place the dish's birth date much earlier. One of these is George Leonard Herter of Waseca, Minnesota, who, among other activities, has written a cookbook in collaboration with his wife called *Bull Cook and Authentic Historical Recipes and Practices.*

Mr. Herter advances the notion that the first chili con carne recipe was written down by a mysterious Spanish nun, Sister Mary of Agreda, who appeared among the Indians in what is now the Southwest of the United States in the seventeenth century. Sister Mary was a very beautiful woman according to those who knew her: "rosy of complexion and large of eye." She entered a convent at Agreda in Castile, near the Aragon border, in 1618 when she was sixteen. About two years later, she began to have "spells." She would go into trances in which her body appeared almost lifeless for days. When she woke up, she would say that her spirit had been transported to a faraway land. There she said her spirit preached Christianity to savages.

It is certain that she never left Spain in the flesh. Still, in the awed belief of some early Spanish missionaries to the New World, and in the firm belief of her friend, King Philip IV of Spain, she was the ghostly "La Dama de Azul," or "The Lady in Blue," who became a legend among Indians of the Southwest.

The Archbishop of Mexico reported to his superiors in Spain that there was a *santa,* or holy woman, in blue habit working among the wild Indians, well in advance of the priests and soldiers. One witness was Father Alonso de Benavides. Between 1621 and 1629, Father Alonso was in charge of a mission at the present site of El Paso, Texas. The padre said that he first heard of The Lady in Blue when some West Texas Indians, the Jumanos, who'd never before known white men, came in and told a strange tale. They said a girl in blue appeared among them and among neighboring tribes and taught them the rudiments of Christianity and told them to seek out the Spanish missionaries for more training.

Father Alonso showed the Jumanos a small painting of a Spanish nun and asked the Indian visitors if The Lady in Blue resembled the picture. "Yes, only she is younger and more beautiful," was the reply.

Other reports came in, including one from the Tiguas of New Mexico (the legend is still current with a fragment of the Tiguas now living in El Paso), and one from the Caddoes, far away in eastern Texas and Louisiana.

Father Alonso returned to Spain in 1631. He was told of the young nun at Agreda who had had those strange visions. Her order wore a blue habit. Father Alonso went to Agreda and had a long interview with Mary, by that time the abbess of her convent.

She described to him people and scenes of the Southwest

wilderness, very vividly, with details she could have never known without being there — at least in spirit. She recited, for example, a detailed physical description of the chief of the group of Jumanos who came to El Paso's site to see the priests.

She convinced Father Alonso and also the King of Spain, who came to visit her four times and corresponded with her for the rest of his life. Perhaps she felt she had created too much of a stir. Anyway, the gentle nun made no more miraculous transmigrations to the New World after the King came for his first visit.

George Leonard Herter in his lively cookbook (which includes what he calls the Virgin Mary's recipe for cooking spinach) credits Mary of Agreda with finding among the seventeenth-century wild Indians and writing down a chili con carne recipe that would pass muster with most chili purists today except that it includes onions and tomatoes. It called for venison or antelope meat for the main vehicle with the flesh of the javelina or wild musk hog serving for the suet.

The International Chili Appreciation Society, a contemporary organization of chili lovers, would like to have Sister Mary of Agreda for a patron saint. Only they've never been able to get more documentation on her, either from Mr. Herter or any other source.

If the Indians of the Southwest were eating chili in the time of the Spanish conquistadors, the fact wasn't recorded by any early explorer. And the descendants of these Indians don't have chili con carne among their native dishes.

During the 1965 session of the New Mexico state legislature, Representative Arencio Gonzales, a Democrat from San Miguel, sponsored a bill to make the chili pepper the official state vegetable. But the pinto bean people, who have a strong lobby in that state, got into the act. Representative John Bigbee, a Republican from Torrance, proposed a floor amendment which also added the frijole, or pinto bean, as an official state vegetable, sharing the honor with the chili pepper. The Estancia Valley, which Mr. Bigbee represented, is one of the largest pinto-bean-producing areas in the Southwest.

"This is the hottest issue yet to come before our legislature, and I don't think we want to have chili without beans," declared Mr. Bigbee. "Pinto beans have saved more lives in New Mexico than the Red Cross, maybe. I would hate to go home and face the people of the Estancia Valley and tell them that this lawmaking body had left the beans out of the chili."

After this speech, Mr. Gonzales' bill, with Mr. Bigbee's amendment, passed unanimously.

4. Poets, Celebrities, and Jailhouse Chili

"The chili is so good. All gone now . . ."
Elizabeth Taylor
writing to
restaurateur Dave Chasen

Bob Pool was once described, admiringly, by one of his not-so-literate friends as "a something seldom kind of a man." Robert Sprinkle Pool certainly is a unique personality. For example, he used to celebrate his birthday by going down to the pound and buying out all the dogs. Friends, to whom he donated the dogs, got so they dreaded for Bob's birthday to come around.

For about a dozen years after World War II, Bob was the high priest of chili con carne in Dallas. His temple was a red-fronted narrow parlor with red-and-white-checkered cloths on the tables.

The Pool place was across the street from the celebrated specialty store Neiman-Marcus. Once, during a mild slump in business at The Store, the big boss of Neiman-Marcus, Stanley Marcus, lectured his sales people: "You all must be living on Bob Pool's chili, the way the customers are backing off from you." This was a reference to the loud breath one acquired from one of Bob's superlative bowls of red, and Mr. Marcus was in a position to know, for he was a frequent patron of the parlor.

Pool heard about Mr. Marcus's remark and took it ill. He dashed off a note to the Neiman-Marcus president: "You run The Store and I'll run my chili joint."

To illustrate the devotion of Pool's clientele, let's take the case of James Henry Hickerson of Dallas when he flew home from Paris, France, in 1951 to attend his daughter's wedding. Colonel Hickerson had been in Paris for months as an intelligence officer on General Eisenhower's SHAPE staff. Did the colonel go home immediately after he landed at the Dallas airport? No — he headed for Bob Pool's chili parlor. He sat down at a table covered with a red-and-white-checkered cloth and spoke in earnest tones to the proprietor: "This is the moment I've been dreaming of all these months. Bring me a bowl of red. No beans. I love my work in Paris. The French are wonderful. My wife is going back with me. Only one thing is wrong so far: no real Texas-style chili."

He had three bowls.

Carlos Ashley, a former poet laureate of Texas, had just returned from a European trip when he composed some verses about a chili maker he had known as a child. Mr. Ashley, the district attorney of Llano County, told of the famous restaurants he had patronized overseas. Then the D.A. rested his case:

> Yet no chef has ever challenged
> The high gastronomic point
> That was mine in early childhood
> In Bob Sears' chili joint.

Will Rogers, the late Oklahoma humorist and film actor, said that he judged a town by the chili it served. He sampled chili in hundreds of little towns, especially in Texas and Oklahoma. He kept a box score. Will finally concluded that the finest chili of his experience was in a small café in Coleman, Texas. The ingredients for this concoction included "mountain oyster from a bull, not a calf, raised on the slopes of the Santa Anna Mountains," mountain oysters being a term for the testicles of an ex-bull. Will Rogers claimed he never met a man he didn't like. Yet he once "cussed out" a California café operator for serving him an inferior bowl of chili.

Dave Chasen, owner of Chasen's restaurant in Beverly Hills, California, probably serves more chili to international celebrities than anyone else.

One night in 1962 I was in Los Angeles and Dave Chasen, a member of the Chili Appreciation Society, which is based in Dallas, invited me to the restaurant to sample the chili. While I was there, Jack Benny called Dave to order ten quarts of chili to be sent to his home. Mr. Chasen showed me dozens of letters and telegrams from famous people praising the chili. These endorsers included personalities ranging from J. Edgar Hoover to James Stewart, and from Mrs. Eleanor Roosevelt to Elizabeth Taylor.

"Elizabeth Taylor loves chili so much — anyway, Chasen's chili," said Dave. "While she was living in Beverly Hills some years ago, she was in here almost every night for a bowl or two. And, of course, you've heard about me sending her frozen chili to Rome during the shooting of the picture *Cleopatra*."

One of the wires from Miss Taylor read: "The chili is so good. All gone now. Please send ten quarts in dry ice to 448 Via Appia Pignatelli. Love and kisses, Elizabeth Taylor."

That evening I began to think that Dave Chasen's idea of a chili supper was something like that once outlined by a former Texas governor, Allan Shivers, who unaccountably doesn't like chili. (It's a wonder he was ever elected with his handicap!) The governor suggested: "Put a pot of chili on the back of the stove to simmer. Let it simmer and simmer. Meanwhile, broil a good sirloin steak. Eat the steak. Let the chili simmer and simmer. Ignore it."

At Chasen's I had a long string of excellent dishes, including a memorable steak. Finally, the waiter fetched in two shallow bowls of steaming red stuff. I am sorry to report, though, that a real chili buff wouldn't give Dave's product a passing grade. It is actually a fine stew, scented with chili powder.

Perhaps you'd like to try Elizabeth Taylor's delight, though. So here is the Chasen recipe:

The ingredients are: ½ pound of pinto beans; 5 cups of canned tomatoes; 1 pound of chopped sweet peppers; 1½ tablespoons of salad oil; 1½ pounds of chopped onions; 2 crushed cloves of garlic; ½ cup of chopped parsley; 1 pound of ground lean pork; 2½ pounds of chili-grind beef chuck; ⅛ cup of chili powder; 2 tablespoons of salt; 1½ teaspoons of black pepper; 1½ teaspoons of cumin seeds; 1½ teaspoons of monosodium glutamate.

Wash the pinto beans and soak them overnight. Simmer in the soaking water until tender. Add tomatoes and simmer for 5 minutes. Sauté the green peppers in salad oil for 5 minutes. Add the onions and cook until tender, stirring often. Add the garlic and parsley. Sauté the pork and beef in butter for 15 minutes. Add the meat to the onion, tomato, and green pepper mixture, stir in the chili powder, and cook for 10 minutes. Then put in the beans and spices and simmer, covered, for 1 hour. Uncover the pot and simmer for another 30 minutes. Skim the grease from the top. That's it. Serves 8.

Isaac Jones, Jr., the butler at the Governor's Mansion of the state of Texas, doubles as chili con carne and enchiladas chef.

"When John Connally was Governor, he and Mrs. Connally and their children loved chili and enchiladas. I cooked chili for them about three times a month and enchiladas more often," said Jones, an ex-Marine who also served as butler and chili chef in the mansion in the administration just before Connally's — that of Price Daniel.

Isaac Jones, incidentally, cooks "Texas-style" enchiladas, which will be described later.

By the arrival of the 1890s, chili con carne had become a standard entree in most jails in the Southwest. Jailhouse cooks learned the same lesson as did the pioneer chili makers, that chili peppers could work wonders with inferior grades of beef. Just as Will Rogers judged a town by the quality of its chili, so veteran wrongdoers came to rate a jail by its "chili score."

Mrs. Clarence A. Maas of Dallas sent me a chili recipe which she said was the best. I published the formula in my daily newspaper column although it differed little from the "original." Then I heard from Smoot Schmid, a former Dallas County sheriff: "That's just my jail chili. In the old days the jailbirds rated my chili the best served behind bars."

Smoot mentioned that he got some national publicity after a food authority, Julia Wright, came to Dallas. She called Smoot Schmid and said that he'd been recommended to her as a chili authority. The sheriff invited her to come down to the jail kitchen and sample a bowl of red. Afterward, Julia Wright wrote: "I've tried the superlative Smoot Schmid chili. This is the best I've ever tasted."

I repeated the ex-sheriff's claims about Dallas County jailhouse chili. And Renwicke Cary, a *San Antonio Light* columnist, stirred up trouble for me by writing:

"Tolbert acknowledges that chili con carne may have originated in San Antonio. Indeed, he stays on solid historical ground until it comes to the matter of jailhouse chili. Then he recklessly makes claims about the superiority of Dallas County jail chili, implying, although not putting it in those words, that our jailhouse chili is inferior. And yet not in nearly forty years of newspapering in San Antonio have I heard anyone else knock the chili served in our jail.

"If a stronger case for our jailhouse chili is needed, we are ready to make it, even though it may entail going out and getting testimonials from former inmates of the jail through the years."

Cary's paragraphs stirred up the San Antonio sheriff, Bill Hauck, and he was quoted in the Renwicke Cary column: "Even though he did it by inference, Tolbert has downgraded our jail chili. And I'm not going to stand by quietly."

Sheriff Hauck said that the next time I was in San Antonio he was going to arrest me, take me to the jail kitchen, and make me eat some chili there. And I would have to say it was better than Dallas jail chili before I would be released.

Hauck never caught me on my San Antonio visits, and now he's out of office.

The Smoot Schmid recipe was published in my *Saturday Evening Post* article. Outside of the howls from San Antonio, the only complaint I got on the Schmid formula was from Herbert C. Wild of Syracuse, New York, who said the chili gave him indigestion.

"It's no wonder they have those jail breaks in Dallas. The prisoners are trying to escape from the chili," said Mr. Wild, who later admitted that he didn't like any highly seasoned food.

Warden H. E. Moore of the Texas prison system says that never in his memory has a condemned man asked for chili con carne for his last meal. Warden Moore thinks this may be so because so much chili, very good chili, is served in the prison system.

In fact, former inmates often write that they are disenchanted with chili "on the outside" and want the prison recipe. These requests come in so frequently that Dr. George Beto, director of the prison system, has had the formula printed for mailing. You might be interested if you run a restaurant, for it calls for 25 pounds of coarsely ground beef, ½ pound of comino, ¼ pound of chili powder, ⅛ pound of paprika, 2 handfuls of crushed dried red chili peppers, ½ pound of finely chopped garlic. This is put in a cooking container, with water to cover, closed tight, and cooked 15 minutes at high heat before stirring. After this, stir and simmer for 30 to 40 minutes. The prison cooks never add water, although they "correct the seasoning to desired strength" in the final 30 minutes of simmering and put in 2 handfuls of monosodium glutamate "for the desired taste balance."

5. The Appreciation Society (International)

"The aroma of good chili should generate rapture akin to a lover's kiss."

Quotation from Joe Cooper
and the motto of the CASI

In 1947, George Haddaway and Jim Fuller founded the Chili Appreciation Society. It is now called the International Chili Appreciation Society, for it has chapters all over the world, including one launched with considerable ceremony in the autumn of 1964 in Mexico City, the fount of chili con carne in the popular mind, yet in truth a "chili desert" until the Appreciation Society did some missionary work.

The headquarters and the parent chapter of this tough-mouthed gourmet association is in Dallas. One of the goals is to improve the quality of chili in restaurants and broadcast Texas-style recipes all over the earth. George Haddaway, the president or international chief chili head, and other zealous members have even resorted to violence when complaints about bad chili in cafés went unheeded.

George Haddaway is the editor of an aviation magazine, *Flight,* and he gets around the nation a lot in his own plane, testing the local chili when he has the stomach for it. In a Houston airport café he was served some alleged chili which he called the worst in his experience. One ingredient of the atrocity was Boston baked beans.

Now the chief chili head is one of those connoisseurs who wants his pinto beans on the side, if at all. The sight of the sweetish Boston baked beans in the bowl was too much for Haddaway's patience. He told the waitress quietly: "Miss, would you have the chef come out here. I want to see him taste this horrible mess."

The chef refused to make an appearance.

George then rose, took the bowl in one hand, opened a swinging door into the kitchen, and threw the bowl in the general direction of the chef, although he didn't hit that worthy.

The chef came out then, mad as a pint of hornets. He called an airport policeman.

George would have gone to jail, probably, if the policeman hadn't been knowledgeable about chili. The officer listened to Haddaway's and the cook's accounts of the affair. The policeman then commended Haddaway and tongue-lashed the chef, declaring that anyone who put Boston baked beans in chili con carne deserved to have bad things happen to him.

George made his peace with the cook and supplied him with directions for making real chili. Since then there have been no complaints about the café from chili heads.

The society's chapters have luncheon or dinner meetings about once a month. Over steaming bowls they discuss missionary endeavors such as sending approved and mimeographed recipes to chili lovers anywhere who are thoughtful enough to include a stamped and addressed envelope in their requests.

One who received a collection of recipes was an army sergeant stationed in Europe. The sergeant wrote that he was in a dreadful situation: He was soon to return home to Oklahoma with a German bride who had a "bitter aversion" to the chili the husband had made for her in his amateurish way. He was afraid her feelings about this might prejudice his chili-loving relatives against his new wife.

The society advised him to test several approved recipes on the poor German girl in the hope one would please her.

The chili missionaries get letters from people all over the world, most of them complaining about the local chili, or about the total lack of it.

Here are some typical letters:

"This state [California] probably has the lousiest chili makers in the nation," wrote Phillip J. Shuler of Acton, California. "The Chili Appreciation Society and its real chili recipes are the answers to my prayers."

Russell L. Brown of Ketchikan, Alaska, said in his letter: "Alaska is the end of the world when it comes to trying to get a decent bowl of chili."

"I haven't found any real chili since I was in Texas in 1942," was the gripe of T. C. Koerber of Norfolk, Nebraska.

Conditions are no better along the Great Lakes, wrote Roy C. Wheeler of Battle Creek, Michigan: "Chili here is not much more than a mildly peppery tomato soup, and I yearn for the real thing."

"We have a brave little band here in Cincinnati who appreciate good chili, and we hope to establish a chapter of your society," said a letter from George J. Sagel of Cincinnati, Ohio.

It takes considerable stenographic work, and the society is a non-dues-paying organization. And yet sending out this chili literature, with members furnishing their own secretarial services, has caused chapters to spring up all over, including several in Europe. Caldrons of chili in dry ice have been air-freighted to chapters in London and in Bonn, Germany.

From Parma, Italy, came the news that "people all over

Italy have translated the recipes in *The Saturday Evening Post* article on your great society, and we have fallen in love with the dish. Chili is now a sensation in this country. We would like badges signifying membership."

A lady new to Texas came into a Dallas restaurant, saw the local chapter in session in a corner of the place, and, at first glance, took this luncheon meeting for a gathering of religious fanatics or political extremists. The men were all standing around a table, mumbling in unison. Arms were outstretched in a kind of double Nazi salute. Later, she learned that she had witnessed the "cracker-crumbling ritual" over steaming bowls with which all chapters start a meal.

The society's bible is a book on chili, now out of print but undoubtedly the first of its kind, written by the late Joe Cooper of Dallas. The complete title is *With or Without Beans; Being a Compendium to Perpetuate the Internationally Famous Bowl of Chili (Texas Style) Which Occupies Such an Important Place in Modern Civilization.*

A quote from Joe Cooper's book is the society slogan: "The aroma of good chili should generate rapture akin to a lover's kiss."

To illustrate how far the society will go in its missionary work, a committee of the international officials from Dallas, including Haddaway, Chief Chili Cook Wick Fowler, and Kitchen Helpers Ted Maloy, David Witts, and Buck Maryyat, flew to Mexico City for "investure" ceremonies for that new chapter. The Mexico City chapter was headed by Pancho Ochoa, an advertising man, and included were such members as Mexico's ambassador to Chile, Chino Ortiz, a former newspaperman.

At the first meeting, about fifty Mexicans were introduced to Texas-style chili and became members of La Sociedad de Aficionados al Chili con Carne (Internacional).

Pepe Romero, author of a column called *"Un Momentito"* in the *Mexico City News*, wrote: *"Viva chili con carne!* La Sociedad de Aficionados al Chili con Carne (Internacional) added at least fifty new members, all of them Mexican *chicos de la prensa*, when the officers of this society from Dallas came to town and set their chief culinary concocter to work. Chief Chili Head Haddaway orated in clear and forceful De Gaulle Spanish." In his address, Haddaway suggested that statesmen of the world should settle dangerous international problems "not in cold conference rooms but over steaming bowls of red." Pepe Romero admitted, after sampling a couple of bowls, that "the propagation of the original recipe and the constant consumption of chili con carne could change the textbook of the humanities."

Romero reported that everyone went back for at least a second helping, and some had four.

Amanda Farga, a Mexico City writer on gourmet foods, said that Fowler's Texas chili was "incomparable." Ambassador Chino Ortiz also called it incomparable. This made Chef Fowler a little uneasy and he said: "You guys keep repeating that word, incomparable. Maybe, you just mean you've never tasted anything before to compare with it."

The Netherlands' Queen Juliana and Prince Bernhard were visiting in Mexico City at the time. And Jorge Rubio, managing director of Hotel Montejo, where the Mexican chili chapter had its first meeting, told Haddaway and Fowler: "You are about the most important fellows in Mexico today, competing for headlines with Queen Juliana and Prince Bernhard."

Now the menu of Restaurant Terraza Caribal in the Hotel Montejo, overlooking the Paseo de la Reforma, lists this entree: "Chili con carne ala Wick Fowler; 18 pesos; pulpa de res en trocitos, condimentos con varios clases de chilis y especias."

And to point up what a good propaganda job the Texas chili missionaries did, a Mexico City magazine printed the recipe as follows:

COPIA FIEL DE LA RECETA ORIGINAL (para doce

personas). Ingredients: 1½ kilgramos de carne molida, no muy fina; un kilogramo de jitomates maduros; una cebolla grande, picada, y dos dientes de ajo finamente picados; una cucharadita de sal, una cucharadita de pimienta roja; una cucharada, al ras, de orégano, y una cucharada de comino; media docena de chilis serranos rojos; cuatro cucharadas de chili en polvo (tipo piquín); una cucharada de paprika.

Forma de prepararse: Se fríe la carne en una sartén, junto con la cebolla y el ajo. Cuando está perfectamente dorada, se le agrega el jitomate molido y un poco de agua. Se añaden los demás ingredientes. Se cubre con dos centímetros de agua y se revuelve muy bien. Se deja hervir a fuego lento hora y media o más, moviéndola regularmente. Ya al final se le añade harina mezclada con agua caliente para espesar.

Nota: en las versiones modernas del chili con carne, se le pone también una cucharidita de salsa tabasco.

Also, in 1964, Haddaway and his helpers prudently obtained all the ingredients for several pots of chili at Hernandez Grocery on Alamo Street in Dallas, and then they set out for Los Angeles to launch ceremoniously the first California chapter.

Matt Weinstock, a Los Angeles newspaper columnist, wrote: "As true aficionados know, the urge for a good bowl of chili con carne can be overwhelming. At last, due reverence has been given to this fiery ambrosia. Amid wild acclaim, the L.A. chapter of the International Chili Appreciation Society was installed at the Airport Marina Hotel.

"Some fun-loving fellows from Dallas, who have kept the Society's fires burning, were here for the occasion. Wick Fowler's chili brought tears to the eyes and perspiration to the brow, but it was so great the memory lingers on.

"The inexperienced should be warned — real chili con carne is not for sissies. Mr. Fowler served what he called 'Two-Alarm Chili.' His 'Four-Alarm Chili' is reputed to open 18 sinus cavities unknown to the medical profession."

The Los Angeles chapter, headed by Doc Bishop, Woody De Silva, Peg Hereford, Bill Hipple, Roy Palmer, Blanche Russell, and Burck Smith, coined a new word, "chilinauts," for the aficionados. And the Los Angeles group also became missionaries. They made a bus trip into the California wine country to launch a new Cucamonga chapter of CASI.

Most society luncheons have a pretty rigid menu: jalapeño peppers for a salad; crackers, and perhaps onions and frijoles on the side. The Californians at Cucamonga had the first chili supper in the society's history in which unlimited quantities of Regina champagne were served along with the bowls of red.

Wick Fowler did some missionary work for the Appreciation Society in Vietnam. Fowler took a temporary war correspondence job with the Denton, Texas, *Record-Chronicle,* and fetched along a big supply of chili peppers and spices to Vietnam.

There he served big pots of Texas-style chili to front line troops.

"I mostly depended on the U.S. Armed Forces for my beef, but I found that water buffalo meat makes magnificent chili," declared Wickford Fowler.

There are always a few "chili haters" around, though, and one of these is Herc Ficklen of Dallas, who commented as follows on Fowler's activities in Vietnam:

"By luring U.S. troops into eating his version of chili, Wick Fowler was aiding and abetting the enemy. Instead he should have been feeding that chili to the Viet Cong."

Chief Chili Head Haddaway came to the defense of Fowler: "Editor Bill Rives [who is, incidentally, poet laureate of the Chili Appreciation Society] has to say that he was simply sending Wick to Vietnam as a war correspondent. The truth is that Fowler was over there mainly on missionary work for our society. Wick's chili will do wonders for our troops' morale. I have two boys in the service, and they may be headed for Vietnam, and I feel better about them now knowing that Wick will see that they get a ration or two of real chili.''

6. Chili in a Can

"The bowl of blessedness!"
Will Rogers' description
of real Texas chili

Most of the chili eaten today in this imperfect world comes from a can. Some of it is pretty terrible, at least by a purist's standards. And yet Gebhardt's of San Antonio, the company which produced the first commercial canned chili in 1908, and such admirable marks as Wolf Brand, Ashley's, Frito, and Ireland's Iron Kettle, still follow classic recipes.

Particularly since 1948, canned chili has been an astounding success story. Figures on production are available only on chili canned in federally inspected plants. In this category, 81.3 million pounds were put in cans in 1948. By 1971 this had increased to 220 million pounds, and the figure now is at least 230 million pounds. This does not include plants engaged only in intrastate business and not obliged to be federally inspected. Since 1951 it has excluded canned chili under contract to the Armed Forces. Also, no statistics are available on "brick chili," produced by thousands of small meat packers for sale in refrigerated meat counters.

Once the canned chili market was mostly in the Southwest. To illustrate the expansion since 1948, Gebhardt's now sells more cans in both the Los Angeles area and New York City than it does in Texas.

Chili-loving oil drill crews from the Southwest are now working all over the earth, and these fellows have had a lot to do with making overseas people familiar with canned chili.

"I can tell when a drilling crew from down here starts to work in, say, the Persian Gulf or Libya or Saudi Arabia — for we start shipping thousands of cases to those places," said Herbert H. Johnson, president of Wolf Brand, which has had its canned chili plant in Corsicana, Texas, since 1921.

When he didn't have time to make his own pot of chili or when he couldn't find a satisfactory bowl in a café, Will Rogers turned to canned chili. His favorite was Wolf Brand.

Once Rogers made a national radio broadcast from Mexico City. He mentioned that he'd searched the Mexican capital in vain for a bowl of red, or "the bowl of blessedness," as he called it. He then commented: "On the way home to Oklahoma I'm going to stop off in Corsicana, Texas, and load up with several cases of Wolf Brand chili so I'll be prepared in the future for emergencies such as this one."

Wolf Brand had humble beginnings. Its founder was a man named Lyman T. Davis. In 1885, Lyman Davis was a land-poor rancher who also owned a meat market in Corsicana. He was a chili head and particularly fond of that produced by a former range cook whose name is no longer remembered. Davis formed a chili-making partnership with the chuck wagon cook, whose recipe put the accent on chunks of lean beef from which he had removed all fat, gristle, and sinew. This artist used rendered beef suet, and his chili was heavily spiced.

Lyman Davis and his dedicated *cocinero* made several caldrons of chili con carne daily and sold it by the pot to cafés. They carried it in a wagon, equipped with a charcoal stove

over which the chili simmered on the trip. Their best customer was the Blue Front Saloon, where it was sold retail for
five cents for a huge bowl with all the crackers you wanted.

Still clinging to the old range cook's formula, although by
that time his partner has passed away, Davis began to can
chili in 1921 in the rear of his meat market. He named his
brand in honor of his pet wolf, Kaiser Bill, and put a likeness
of Bill on each can.

At first he turned out only two hundred cans a day. Then
he began to produce cans by the thousands in a plant. Davis
was a shrewd salesman. To grocers who sold his product well
during the year, he would return a "bonus," sometimes as
much as five hundred dollars. Naturally, the grocers began to
push Wolf Brand.

He had salesmen all over the Southwest, and they traveled
in Model T Fords. The cabs, or passenger compartments, of
these coupes were shaped from the windshield header up like
a can of chili and were decorated with a picture of a wolf and
signs which read "The Famous Wolf Brand Chili." In the
cargo compartment were cages containing lives wolves, or, in
some cases, coyotes when the wolf crop was low.

These were amiable, well-fed-looking beasts, and it was
mentioned by the salesmen that the wolves' diet included
liberal portions of Wolf Brand chili.

Lyman Davis left the company in the 1920s. His ranch had
become so densely planted in oil wells that he had to sell Wolf
Brand and devote full time to the business of being a
millionaire.

Today Wolf Brand, a member of the Quaker Oats family,
turns out canned chili by the millions of cans. It is still made
by the old range cook's formula, and the labels still bear the
picture of Kaiser Bill, the pet wolf.

7. The Chili Powder Men

"The health-giving properties of hot chili peppers have no equal."

DeWitt Clinton Pendery,
pioneer chili powder manufacturer

Preparing the chili peppers for making chili con carne in the original manner is an arduous task, and it can be painful if any of the alkaloid fire in the veins of the pods comes in contact with a cut on your hand.

Chili con carne was seldom made by home cooks until the 1890s. Then either William Gebhardt of New Braunfels, the founder of the great Gebhardt's canned chili company, or DeWitt Clinton Pendery of Fort Worth invented chili powder.

New Braunfels, just east and almost a suburb of San Antonio now, was begun in 1845 by a colony of Germans under the leadership of Prince Karl of Solms-Braunfels. You can still see the machine with which in 1896 William Gebhardt ground chili powder from dried ancho pods. Actually, this powder was a complete chili seasoning, for he ground orégano, cumin seeds, and garlic in with the chili pods.

54

Thus the housewife was given a simple, quick way to make chili con carne. Chili would never have gained wide acceptance if it hadn't been for the "powder men." The memory of William Gebhardt and DeWitt Clinton Pendery was honored at the 1972 World Series of Chili in Terlingua, Texas.

William Gebhardt moved his operations to San Antonio in 1896 and canned the first commercial chili there in 1908. The Gebhardt Company has the founder's original chili powder-grinding machine on display. Yet the company has few facts on the life of William Gebhardt. He sold out early to a brother-in-law and disappeared from the "chili scene."

Ramsdell and Cooper, the only other chili historians I know, give Gebhardt the credit for making the first chili powder. It may be, though, that DeWitt Clinton Pendery was the first to achieve this milestone in gastronomy.

Pendery was a well-dressed, well-educated man of thirty-two when he arrived in Fort Worth in 1870 from his native Cincinnati, Ohio. He didn't receive a hospitable reception. When he alighted from the stagecoach, a bemused cowboy shot off the visitor's tall silk stovepipe hat.

Today, Pendery's daughter-in-law, Mrs. Arthur Ludlow Pendery of Fort Worth, still has the stovepipe hat with the bullet holes in the crown. It is a treasured reminder of the courage of her father-in-law. For, on that day in 1870, Mr. Pendery calmly picked up his hat from the dusty Fort Worth street, adjusted it casually, and went on his way, unhurriedly.

His coolness aroused the admiration of the local marksmen, who often thus met stagecoaches and "initiated" male newcomers into the quaint mores of Fort Worth. (This wasn't as tough as the initiation ceremony then conducted in some ports on the Texas side of the Red River, where jokesters made newcomers drink a hatful of the highly mineralized waters of that crimson stream before they were formally granted admittance into Texas.)

D. C. Pendery, who died in 1924, is almost canonized today

among chili lovers of North Texas. In 1890 he started a pungent institution in Fort Worth, still operated by his descendants, called Mexican Chili Supply Company, first spelled "chilley."

In 1870 he had set up as a groceryman in Fort Worth. In the 1880s he began to note that a large number of his customers asked for chili peppers and spices for making chili con carne, for hot tamales, and for thin, long corn shucks in which tamales are cooked.

His store burned down in 1890. And the elegant Yankee from Cincinnati, who was, nevertheless, a chili and tamale fancier, decided to devote his whole business to supplying pepper pods and spices for chili and tamales. In that same year, according to his advertisements, he started grinding an excellent blend of chili powder, which he called "chilomaline," from pepper pods and orégano, cumin seeds, and garlic.

This powder blend is still made. As has the chili supply house today, D. C. Pendery always had on hand immense supplies of ancho chilies, large of pod and sold by the bale or half-dozen; chilipiquines, which he wrote as "chilequinpins," and many other peppers, such as the burning-hot *mambasa* from Africa, and Mexican garlic, Spanish paprika, comino, orégano, coriander seeds, tamarind, bay leaves. Still on sale are *piloncillos,* Mexican sugar loaves. And sometimes old men who have been customers for decades slip in to buy the thinnest of corn husks in which to roll cigarettes.

One of old Mr. Pendery's "hobbies" was donating the spices for Fort Worth firemen to make what came to be called "fire-hall chili."

Pendery catered to hotel restaurants and to cafés all over the United States, and he sought to improve the quality of the nation's chili by sending out excellent printed recipes to the chefs. He also dispatched directions for tamales, enchiladas, a relish called "chili-carow," and chili-marcaroni.

Of course, he knew nothing about the heavy Vitamin A

and C content in fresh chili peppers or preserved ones, yet this imaginative salesman wrote in his advertising, as early as 1891, that the peppers were beneficial to health. In one of these advertisements he said: "We desire to call to the attention of chili con carne and tamale makers, especially those throughout the north and middle states, that cold weather months are not the exclusive months for making the chili and tamale business profitable. Am judging this by this business house's experience in supplying the trade. We have found that the spring and summer months are most profitable in the southern states.

"We make this known from the fact that a great many who have built up a trade in the north and middle states invariably drop the business when warm weather approaches, and then take it up again in the fall. This is a great mistake because dishes such as chili con carne, tamales, enchiladas, etc., when properly prepared and served, act as a tonic upon the system, such as is usually demanded throughout the hot climates of tropical America.

"It is well said by one of our most prominent physicians that few persons appreciate the benefits to be derived from the use of 'chilimaline' [his chili powder blend]. The health-giving properties of hot chili peppers have no equal. They give tone to the alimentary canal, regulating the functions, giving a natural appetite, and promoting health by action on the kidneys, skin, and lymphatics."

Whether he was the innovator of chili powder or not, DeWitt Clinton Pendery deserves a prominent place in the history of chili con carne.

8. "Greaseless Chili"

"Chili just isn't chili without a little grease."
International Chief Chili Head
George Haddaway

Richard M. McLean, a San Francisco advertising executive, wrote me a sad letter: "I've had a severe heart attack. I'm now completed recovered, yet I know my chili-eating days are over."

At the same time I heard from a Dallas friend, Chevus Chapman, a young bank president, who'd also had a massive heart attack but was healthy again, only very cautious about his diet: "I'll miss chili more than any other food."

Also, a Las Vegas, Nevada, member of the Chili Appreciation Society wrote: "My mother-in-law is the most voracious chili eater I know about. Yet she has developed an allergy to suet. .She's going crazy on a non-chili diet. What shall I do?"

I got off "greaseless," nonsuet recipes to these three. Their doctors approved of the formula, just as did President Johnson's medicine man after his heart attack.

58

I haven't gotten a progress report on the Las Vegas mother-in-law. But Mr. McLean of San Francisco and Mr. Chapman of Dallas are again happy chili eaters and they say it has improved their morale no end.

International Chief Chili Head Haddaway once threatened to kick me out of the Appreciation Society if I didn't quit "going around advocating greaseless chili."

Haddaway lectured me: "The original Texas-style chili had grease in it. Chili just isn't chili without a little grease."

"Yes, sir. Yes, sir, your chief chili headship," I replied, but I went on passing out greaseless chili recipes.

Since then something has happened — maybe some people began to get high cholesterol counts — anyway, Haddaway and the rest of the parent chapter have quit crusading against greaseless chili. As recited in the first chapter, the chief cook, Wick Fowler, leaves the suet out and spoons for grease even when he's using the leanest meat he can find.

The only chili I've ever cared for in which the beans were cooked with the meat was something styled "Arizona greaseless chili," served in the years just before World War II by the Womack family in the old Delta Café in Fort Worth.

The pinto beans were cooked in the normal way, although without salt. When tender, they were worked into a paste in a blender. The meat was round steak, broiled until rare, and then put in the refrigerator overnight, after which the grease was spooned off. The cold beef was cut into cubes less than a half inch in diameter. The pinto bean paste and the cubed rare steak were then simmered in a minimum of water with chili pepper pulp or chili powder and the other spices until done.

Mrs. Cora Lee Tompkins, who lives in a beautiful seaside villa on Texas' most lovely shore, southern Padre Island, off Brownsville, is famous for her greaseless chili.

It is pretty much like Pedernales River chili, except that in the Padre Island version even more pains are taken to get all the grease out of the leanest venison or beef.

Mrs. Tompkins usually makes it with three pounds of venison and one pound of venison sausage. The venison sausage is fried until browned and completely separated, then it is dipped from the skillet with a slotted spoon and drained on paper towels.

The three pounds of venison are also seared and laid on the paper towels to drain off grease.

The next step is to put the venison in the big iron skillet with the spare sausage drippings and stir until well heated. The drained sausage then joins the venison in the skillet with just enough water to cover. Let it come to a boil and then simmer for one hour.

If Mrs. Tompkins suspects that there still may be a bit of grease in the meat, she lets the mixture cool and sets it in the icebox for the fat to rise and be skimmed off. Her directions call for one can of Gebhardt's Chili Quick, but you can use the same chili pepper pulp and spices mentioned in the first chapter.

Mrs. Tompkins adds cracker meal for thickening, but Masa Harina would do just as well.

The chili is then simmered until the meat is done and the spices have had time to blend. This serves eight.

9. The Scene of the Chili Wars

"In a lifetime spent in traveling, here I came upon the greatest wonder. The mantle of God touches you ... it is panorama without beginning or end ..."
Ludwig Bemelmans
on the Big Bend

Terlingua, Texas, is on shelves of mauve gravel, sparsely planted in cacti and other desert botany, with little arroyos in between the more or less level pitches of gravel. The spooky-looking village is in southern Brewster County and about ten miles inboard from the grand canyons of the Rio Grande.

In land mass, Brewster County is bigger than the combined provinces of Connecticut and Rhode Island, and yet there are only about seven thousand people living in the county, most of them in two towns in the northern reaches, Alpine and Marathon. Terlingua is about eighty miles south of Alpine and about ten miles west of an entrance to Big Bend National Park.

In downtown Terlingua there is a continuous block of buildings, composed of adobe and stone and concrete, the block about fifty yards long and fronted by a wide, high concrete gallery. Included in this block is the Chisos Oasis, a former saloon and dance hall, still in a good state of preservation. Just next to the Oasis is the thick-walled yet roofless opera house. Back of the business buildings, up the slope toward Cigar Mountain, there is a classic little church, still in use. And off to the west of the downtown are the ruins of an ornate mansion, once the command post of a rather mysterious financier named Howard Perry.

For many years Howard Perry was the owner and virtual ruler of Terlingua and its Chisos (sometimes translated as "ghost") cinnabar mine.

Terlingua is in a weird setting, one of geologically savage beauty, 788,682 acres of it preserved as wilderness in the Big Bend National Park. This land is called the Big Bend because it is there that the Rio Grande makes a four-hundred-mile abrupt turn from its normal southward flow to, finally, almost due north through mountains eight thousand feet high on the U.S. side and higher on the Mexican shores. And near Terlingua the river flows lustily through awesome, narrow gorges, sometimes between sheer cliffs two thousand feet high.

In the 1840s a cowboy, who must have been something of a poet, was asked directions from a traveler bound into the Terlingua country. The cowboy said: "You go south from Fort Davis until you come to place where the rainbows wait for the rain and the mountains float in the air, except at night when they go away to play with other mountains. And the river is kept in big, stone boxes and water rolls uphill . . ."

The Chisos Mountains *do* sometimes seem to float up out of the mirages in the surrounding painted deserts. And there are often profusions of rainbows when there are showers in the mountains, and the strange structural patterns of the cliffs in the river canyons sometimes make it appear the Rio Grande is flowing uphill.

A European artist and writer, Ludwig Bemelmans, fell into superlatives while writing in a 1958 national magazine article about the Big Bend: "In a lifetime spent in traveling, here I came upon the greatest wonder. The mantle of God touches you; it is what Beethoven reached for in music; it is panorama without beginning or end. No fire can burn so bright, no projection can duplicate the colors that dance over the desert or the bare rock formations that form the backdrop. No words can tell you, and no painter hold it. It is only to be visited and looked at with awe. It will make you breathe deeply whenever you think of it, for you have inhaled eternity."

To Tolbert, who has been prowling around in the Big Bend since childhood, this wild land is like a stage, as big as New England, in which the fascinating scenes change with each new slant of the ardent sun or with every movement of clouds and morning fogs. Old Ludwig Bemelmans may have been watching the setting sun bouncing colors off the painted walls of the Carmen Mountains, or gazing on the phallic-shaped outer peaks of the Chisos rising suddenly four thousand feet out of the desert floor. (H. Allen Smith, to whose dim eye the Big Bend landscape is "mostly rancid," says that Ludwig Bemelmans must have been boozing it up when he wrote so poetically about the Texas wilderness.)

A historian, Walter Prescott Webb, said he was always "homesick" for the Big Bend country when he was away from what "could never be my home." He also wrote one of the best capsule descriptions of its geological aspect: "There it lies in all its gorgeous splendor and geological confusion, almost as if it fell from the hands of its Creator. It fascinates because it seems to be made up of the scraps left over when the world was made, containing samples of rivers, deserts, blocks of sunken mountains, and then tree-clad peaks, dried-up lakes, canyons, cuestas, vegas, playas, arroyos, volcanic refuse, and hot springs . . ."

Until recent years when the surrounding 220,000-acre ranch was sold and turned over to land "developers" who cut it up into "ranchettes," Terlingua was probably the most satisfactory ghost town on the Rio Grande. Even today the town looks a little like a big and abandoned Indian pueblo, with many roofless adobe and stone buildings blending in mauve and yellow colors with the spiky landscape and the usually iridescent sky.

Once Terlingua was the capital of the richest quicksilver mining country in the U.S. For example, in 1922, 40 percent of the cinnabar in this country was mined there.

One story is that Howard Perry, who was from Portland, Maine, bought for $150 the 1,280 acres encompassing the future townsite of Terlingua and the mines from Richard M. Gano, surveyor, preacher, and ancestor of Howard Hughes. (General Gano surveyed much of the Big Bend originally. He preached as he surveyed and traded in land. One of the daily entries from his diary reads: "Today I saved 20 souls and sold 16 sections of land.")

Old Man Perry was proud of his town in its heyday. He was a man of slight statue. The climate of Terlingua is quite sunny, even in midwinter. And while there Mr. Perry appeared each day in a fresh white linen suit and he usually wore a flat straw hat with a vivid bow.

Sometime early in this century Mr. Perry bought a red motorcar called a Columbia. Some Columbias were electrically impelled, but not this one. It had a four-cylinder engine, cast in two blocks with two cylinders in each block and driven by dual chains.

Mr. Perry parked the Columbia in an adobe garage and had it sealed in there after he'd driven the car only a few miles. Then he probably forgot about the vehicle. For during World War II times, when mercury was again being mined in Terlingua, the Columbia was found sealed in the adobe chamber and still in mint condition except that its rubber had rotted. A collector of classic automobiles bought the Columbia and won first place in one of the Glidden Tours with the former property of the forgetful czar of early Terlingua.

Perry would sit on one of the wide galleries of his twenty-room mansion and recite: "When I came here there was only me and two jackasses. Now look at what I've created!"

Howard Perry had another twenty-room mansion on the bay at Cumberland Foreside, Maine, and at one time he owned a two-masted schooner which required a crew of eight.

Bruce Roberts, a columnist for the Portland, Maine, *Evening Express*, once lived near the Perry estate at Cumberland Foreside, and Mr. Roberts wrote that "Perry was just as much a mystery figure in Maine as in Terlingua. Only a lucky few were invited for an afternoon cruise." (In a 1968 letter to me, Perry's nephew, John Merrell of Portland, objected to this description: "My uncle was from Cleveland and his wife from Chicago. They came to live on this Maine bay because he liked sailing. What's mysterious about that?")

Anyway, during his long years in Terlingua, Howard Perry discouraged visitors to his little kingdom, especially if they were "government men." It was usually so hot in the shafts that the miners worked in the nude. Mr. Perry ran everything from the police force to the school board. And he built a thick-walled jail with steel rings in the sides of the walls for fastening chains. This dungeon, next to the now roofless opera house, is still in good condition.

"No one ever broke out of Señor Perry's Jail," I was told in 1964 by Marcario Hinojas, a Seminole Indian then eighty-five years old and living rent free in one of the abandoned adobe houses in Terlingua. Marcario said he went to work in the Perry mines in 1908 and when the mines finally closed down after World War II the old Indian went to work as a pack mule handler in the Big Bend park.

The original Terlingua was down near where Terlingua Creek and its satellite stream, Dirty Woman Creek, run into the Rio Grande. And it was probably called Tres Lingos, for the three languages spoken at an early Indian trading post, Spanish, English, and Comanche. This was the court language of this country, although it was primarily Apache land.

By the time Howard Perry established his town near the mines, Tres Lingos had been corrupted into Terlingua.

It is said there is still plenty left in the Terlingua lode, but cinnabar can be produced so much more cheaply in foreign lands that the mines aren't worth working except in wartime.

All this is leading up to the fact that, beginning in the autumn of 1967, Terlingua became the site for the annual World's Chili Cookoff. The idea for the competition was Tolbert's and Tom Tierney's. And, in a way, we started a worldwide subculture, for there are now more than one thousand annual cookoffs.

The first edition of the book you are now reading had come out the year before and had revived interest in chili con carne. Several national magazines carried their first articles on chili. And the cookoff at Terlingua was designed as a prankish promotion for *A Bowl of Red*.

I'd been off in Beverly Hills, sampling Dave Chasen's tame chili again — just to be polite. And the original idea was for Mr. Chasen, Elizabeth Taylor's official chili cook, to be matched against the chief cook of the Chili Appreciation Society International, the great Wick Fowler.

The things that recommended Chasen were his national reputation as a restaurateur and the fact that he represented a "chili school" so foreign to the Texas cult. And, best of all, the Beverly Hills restaurateur said something about bringing Elizabeth Taylor to Terlingua as his second at the cookoff.

However, with the date for the competition only a few weeks away, Mr. Chasen became ill.

We had to find someone else to cook against the CASI champion. As if by a miracle a contender of the Chasen class appeared. He was H. Allen Smith, author of many humor books, such as *Low Man on a Totem Pole*, who was at the time living on a milking goat farm near Mount Kisco, New York.

Tierney operates possibly the most live-wire public relations firm in Dallas. He called my attention to an article written by H. Allen Smith in the August 1967 issue of *Holiday* magazine — the article full of anti-Texas ravings and titled "Nobody Knows More About Chili Than I Do."

"This Smith character will be perfect to meet Wickford in the cookoff," said Tom.

I agreed. The theme of Smith's churlish, three-thousand-word tantrum was (1) Texans can't cook chili, and (2) Smith can. Also the Smithsonian recipe, as published in *Holiday*, was even worse than Chasen's by Texan standards. It was a chili-flavored, low-torque, beef and vegetable soup. Among the ingredients were sweet bell peppers, canned tomatoes, and a lot of onions, and he cooked kidney beans right in with the mess.

Ordinarily an article such as Smith's, with its braggy title, would have created only a mild stir in the late summer lethargy of Texas chili heads and, as Gary Cartwright wrote later in *Sports Illustrated*, would have been "dismissed as an example of Eastern stupidity."

"It'll be kind of like a wrestling match: our hero, Wick Fowler, against the Eastern bad-mouther of Texas chili, a real villain, H. A. Smith," said Tierney.

The only trouble was that I incurred Smith's hostility with my review of his *Holiday* article in my daily column: "Mr. Smith borrows freely from my book, *A Bowl of Red*, and from Charles Ramsdell's admirable book on San Antonio. Only Smith twists and changes his borrowed material. For example, Mr. Smith quotes Ramsdell that chili con carne was originated by the Canary Islanders who were the first civilian settlers in San Antonio. What Ramsdell really said was that chili probably originated in San Antonio among 'the very poorest class of the populace.' Ramsdell never said anything about the proud and usually not especially poor colonists from the Canary Islands inventing chili."

Smith wrote an abusive letter to me in which he not only refused to cook against a member of the Chili Appreciation Society International (he styled CASI members a bunch of "childish, semi-rumped Rotarian cracker-breakers, withered and pockmarked from eating that mud puddin' Texans choose to call chili . . ."), but he also said that he was gathering up all the copies of my chili book he could find in New York and was going to burn them on the public square in Mount Kisco.

He also declared: "I cannot hold still for the imputation that I purloined material from your sleazy chili book and misrepresented facts from Charles Ramsdell's history of San Antonio. You lie! You fib!

"I got word from my New York agent that I'd been challenged to a duel," Smith wrote. "Wickford P. Fowler of Austin, Texas, had flung down the gauntlet and offered to cook chili against me. I responded that I would not be drawn into combat with trash.

"Fowler, in collaboration with the varlet, X. Tolbert, launched a torrent of abuse against me, charging me with arrant chickenhood, saying I had taken to my bed with the Buff Orpington syndrome. I was in a deep fury; my deep fealty to the middle western concept of chili had been wounded; the storied honor of the Illinois Smiths [H. Allen was born in Iron Stob, Illinois] had been impugned. I notified X. Tolbert that if I could locate a horsewhip I was coming to Dallas and horse whip him in front of his Dallas *News* colleagues. I added that as long as I would have to pay for the airline fare, it would be my pleasure while in Dallas to horsewhip any other Texans who pretend to a knowledge of chili . . ." This was the gracious way Old H.A. accepted Wick's challenge to compete in the first, or 1967, cookoff.

I told Smith to be prepared to start cooking at high noon. This set the old boy to raving:

"High noon! A fitting hour for treachery! Gary Cooper had no one but Colby and Pearce and the black-hearted Miller brothers to vanquish at his high noon encounter. I have 209 childish lardheads [he meant the high officials of the CASI] and a houseboat jockey [Fowler builds houseboats as a hobby] to defeat . . ."

In his *Sports Illustrated* article on the first cookoff, Gary Cartwright seemed to think Smith had fallen into a trap: "Texans for historical reasons believe that any chili that isn't theirs is trickery . . ." And Cartwright said that Texans might even react violently to the "fresh tomatoes, sweet bell peppers, and other ingredients of Smith's school of chili. CASI is a self-appointed police force against such practices . . . Smith's attraction was that he fixed his name onto a magazine article titled 'Nobody Knows More About Chili Than I Do.' From a hook that large, CASI could hang a Brahman bull. When Smith allowed himself to be coerced from his home in Mount Kisco, New York, to the ghost town of Terlingua, Texas, in the remote Big Bend country — there to cook burner to burner against CASI's chief cook, Wick Fowler — he had played into the hands of the enemy . . . Only foolish pride or an incurable dope habit would force a man into this country (the Big Bend) to take a chance he knew he didn't have. CASI didn't care which it was with H. Allen Smith . . ."

Maury Maverick, Jr., a member of one of Texas' most distinguished families and a San Antonio attorney, had Smith as a house guest several months before the first cookoff. When he read Smith's article in *Holiday*, though, Maverick wrote a letter to the editor of the San Antonio *Express* containing bitter adverse criticism of the Smith recipe, especially of the sweet bell peppers which H. Allen urged *Holiday* magazine readers to include.

Smith lost some of his arrogance when he read the Maverick letter. And he took the strange ploy of claiming that he was "brainwashed" by his wife into putting the bell peppers into his chili pot. In a letter to the editor of the San Antonio *Express*, Smith said:

"I never do anything for which I have to apologize. Always when it appears I've committed an evil act there are extenuating circumstances. I didn't remember that I'd included sweet bell peppers in the chili recipe published in *Holiday*."

Smith then made the shameless claim that his wife sneaks into the kitchen when he's not around and drops bell peppers into his chili pot, in addition to brainwashing him into putting the sweet peppers in his published recipes.

"I once became so desperate about this situation that I shopped all over New York City for a Dutch oven equipped with a hasp and padlock (washable).

"I figured on getting the chili prepared and then locking the damned pot against her. But I couldn't even find a pressure cooker that could be locked down. A pox on the hardware trade, right up to and including Hammacher Schlemmer.

"As you well know it has long been fashionable for men to work themselves to death for their women, leaving their wives in the lap of luxury. [Editor's note: Smith coined that phrase 'lap of luxury.'] Well, I have an intense desire to outlive my wife. I want it to be that way for one reason. It is my hope that in my final years I will be able to make a pot of chili without any sweet bell peppers in it . . ."

10. The First Cookoffs

"If you drink tequila don't dive off the front gallery. Most generally the water is too low. Besides they is a $10 fine."

Original sign in
Terlingua's Chisos Oasis Saloon

When Tom Tierney and I conceived the idea of the World Series of Chili, we didn't figure it would be well attended because of the isolation of Terlingua, which is eighty miles from the nearest real town. We first believed that one big chartered plane from Dallas and one from Los Angeles (where the chili heads are unusually active) would take care of everyone who wanted to go.

In his "chili column" for the San Antonio *Express,* Maury Maverick also expressed concern that not many of the members of CASI chapters would bother to go to Terlingua and those who did attend would be, to quote roughly from Shakespeare, "we happy few . . . we band of brothers . . ."

As things turned out, 209 chapters of the Chili Appreciation Society from all over the United States were represented, some coming in jets, some in four-motored prop planes, some in DC-3s, plus at least twenty smaller aircraft, and many motoring to the cookoff.

Mrs. Harold Wynne, wife of the Chiracahua Ranch foreman, gets her mail at Terlingua although the ranch headquarters is off in the Christmas Mountains, thirty-five miles by wheeled vehicle to the post office, seventeen miles of it over a dreadful road through the desert which Dave Witts calls the "Terlingua Autobahn."

Mrs. Audra Wynne is a superb cook and is interested in cookery. Yet after the first cookoff she has chosen to absent herself from the Terlingua scene when the chili heads are there.

"The reason is that the first cookoff you threw here caused Audra to have a nervous breakdown," Harold Wynne told me. "It was them Californians that fretted her most, such as that mean rascal of a monk and the California champion chili maker, 'Wino Woody.' But some of the Texans cut up pretty mean, too, while they were guests at the ranch."

Carroll's Shelby's two-motored plane was the first to arrive for the 1967 cookoff. Shel brought along two dozen or so folks from California, including two good-looking Swedish girls and a man identified as "Father Duffy" and dressed in medieval robes and crude sandals.

Shelby's plane landed at the crude airstrip of the Chiracahua Ranch headquarters. Many of the people who came to the first cookoff stayed at the Chiracahua, for there were no proper accommodations then at Terlingua.

Gary Cartwright in his *Sports Illustrated* report said that "Father Duffy arrived fortified with two women friends." He was referring to the fair Swedes, in truth friends of Carroll Shelby, then a bachelor. Father Duffy was actually an imposter, a usually sedate young California businessman and married. It seems he only wears monk's robes to chili cookoffs. His wife raised the dickens when she read *Sports Illustrated's* text suggesting the bogus monk brought a brace of girl friends to Terlingua.

Cartwright and H. Allen Smith provided some highly interesting inaccuracies in their reports on the first cookoff. For example, neither Maury Maverick nor I was on the road between Alpine and Terlingua that morning. I'd been on a boat trip on the Rio Grande and Maury had been in the Chisos Mountains. Yet Smith had this to say about his journey from Alpine to the scene of the cookoff: "We headed south from Alpine and about five miles out I thought I saw Maury Maverick and Frank Tolbert skulking behind a clump of claret-cup cactus near the highway. I couldn't figure out any kind of ambush they might be planning, so I assumed they had been shooting craps . . . Tolbert owns a pair of dice that have a peculiar tendency to *lean* before settling in place. We sped on our way to Terlingua . . ."

Through Dr. Brownie McNeill, the president of Sul Ross State Teachers College in Alpine, I'd arranged for some school buses to transport the chili heads from the Chiracahua headquarters (where many spent the night out of doors in sleeping bags) to Terlingua. Cartwright wrote that one of the school buses "barely missed running over a mountain lion." Now there are some cougars in this country, but none so awkward as to come down in the desert and almost get hit by a slow-moving bus.

H. A. Smith was more accurate when he described the arrival of the school buses that morning in Terlingua: "A bus came chugging into the Terlingua compound and a good portion of the aristocratic membership of the Chili Appreciation Society International began unloading. They were unshaven, red-eyed, and trying hard not to be sullen. It may have been imagination, but my nostrils picked up goat smell." The Smithsonian nose was correct. The night before, after some of the delegates had drunk their fill and settled in their bedrolls, some out of doors and some in a big stone garage under the ranch house, I had the herders run some Spanish goats over the sleepers, just to make the night exciting. And the scrimmaging between the goats and the suddenly awakened chili heads was particularly spirited in the big garage.

One of the cowboys also disturbed the delegates by galloping his cutting horse around in the narrow lanes between sleeping bags out in the ranch yard. The people in the garage were spared this thrill.

At the start of the 1967 tournament, Master of Ceremonies Bill Rives (who is also the poet laureate of the CASI) tried to present Smith with a proclamation from Governor John Connally making H. Allen an honorary citizen of Texas.

Smith refused rudely, saying: "I have no plans to behave in any honorable way during my stay in Texas."

A true prophecy.

The judges at the first cookoff were David Witts, mayor of Terlingua; Floyd Schneider, a Lone Star Brewery executive from San Antonio; and Justice of the Peace Hallie Stillwell of Alpine. In his *Sports Illustrated* piece, Gary Cartwright declared that Mrs. Stillwell's "court is in Hell's-Half-Acre, Texas . . . It was much later that CASI learned that she is H. Allen Smith's cousin." Now Hell's-Half-Acre is actually thirteen acres of ornery pastureland on the Gage Holland Ranch in Brewster County, so rugged Mr. Holland can't cross-fence, but there's no town or seat for a court there. And Mrs. Stillwell is no blood relation of Smith, although she has been his most loyal friend since he became a resident of Alpine and bruised feelings there by repeatedly being quoted in national magazines and on a television talk show that "there are more greedy, money-grubbing sons-of-bitches per capita in Alpine, Texas, than in any other town I've seen or heard about."

Although the cooking wasn't to start until noon, Smith arrived more than two hours early. He seemed nervous and he was wearing a sidearm. Later he claimed that a shot was fired back of the saloon soon after he arrived on the Chisos Oasis veranda. No one else heard the shot.

Wickford Fowler looked sleepy when he appeared on the

saloon front gallery about 11:30 A.M. He had good reason for his tired look after spending the night at a ranch head-quarters where the other guests included Father Duffy, Woodruff "Wino Woody" De Silva, the California champ (who didn't compete in '67), and other rowdy spirits.

Also, no one ever slept late at the Chiracahua Ranch headquarters. For Foreman Wynne is much given to arous-ing guests at the ranch before dawn with shouts: "Get up! It don't take long to spend the night at the Chiracahua!"

What Smith didn't know at the time was that Maverick, tired of H. Allen's insults, had declined to serve as a judge. Tolbert was retained as referee over Smith's objections.

Fowler and Smith had their pots set up on gas burners on the veranda. Since the sight and sound (and smell) of two men puttering over their chili pots for two hours or so would soon tire the spectators, there was a band of music playing. And Maggie Cobos — Maggie is a man — the Big Bend's leading chuck wagon cook, served to the spectators the cowboys' favorite entree, son-of-a-bitch stew, and barbecued cabrito, or young goat.

When the time came to test the chili, the three judges were blindfolded, although the blindfolds weren't necessary since the judges knew Smith's recipe called for kidney beans while Fowler's classic Texas formula was all beef and seasonings.

Fowler's chili was labeled No. 2 by the referee and Smith's No. 1, or rather that was how the judges were to refer to the different pots. In opinion of some real experts who tasted from the pot later, Fowler cooked magnificent chili, some of the maestro's very best.

Smith's was about as expected. Elizabeth Taylor would have loved it.

Judge Stillwell was the first to taste. She ate several spoon-fuls of the Fowler chili with obvious relish. She took one tiny, bean-filled bite from the Smith pot. Then she proved her friendship to the man from Mount Kisco, New York: "I vote for Soupy's — I mean I vote for No. 1."

Judge Schneider was next. He took a good bite from Smith's pot and tried to retain his composure but failed. Then the San Antonio connoisseur gobbled greedily of Fowler's chili. He voted for Wick.

Last to taste was Judge Witts. He never got around to Fowler's chili. He took one mouthful of the Smith composition. His faced reddened and contorted. He seemed to go into convulsions and fell to the floor of the veranda.

When Mayor Witts was helped to his feet, he finally found voice and he declared his taste buds had been paralyzed by the shock of tasting and swallowing Smith's concoction. With his taste buds allegedly not functioning he said it would be impossible for him to cast the decisive vote.

So there was nothing the referee could do but declare a draw. Fowler was robbed. He deserved to win easily.

Smith had some uncomplimentary things to say about Judges Witts and Schneider: "This Schneider, a hired gun, pressed into service replacing Maury Maverick . . . was a specimen that anthropologists would have rejected. Both he and David Witts were unshaven and bleary-eyed after what must have been a night of sin at the ranch . . . On the other hand Hallie Stillwell was clear-eyed and alert. And cleanshaven."

There were perhaps one thousand spectators at the first cookoff, as contrasted with five thousand to twenty thousand in more recent cookoffs. Yet those thousand people at the '67 tournament were pretty noisy and there was a band of music playing some of the time. And yet Smith claimed he heard a coyote wailing off toward Cigar Mountain and Fred Pass when the judges' decision was announced.

No one else heard the coyote unless it was Cartwright.

In Cartwright's account, he said he didn't know which chili pot caused Witts's alleged accident. Witts said he sampled only "Soupy's pot" and all other eyewitnesses and printed accounts (except Smith's) agreed with Witts's version.

H. Allen Smith and Wick Fowler were supposed to continue their chili war in the 1968 cookoff. Only Smith came down with a case of the hives and had to bow out.

Woodruff De Silva, a distinguished airport consultant and the designer and former director of the Los Angeles International Airport, was brought in to take Smith's place in the duel with Wickford P. Fowler.

Mr. De Silva is Chief Chili Head of the Cucamonga, California, chapter of the Chili Appreciation Society International. He is known as "Wino Woody" because he is very partial to champagne. He drinks champagne copiously as he cooks chili, and he was fresh from repeating as California state chili champion when he came to Terlingua for the 1968 cookoff.

One thing for sure, Woody De Silva is the all-time pickle champion of the Los Angeles County Fair. In the 1971 fair, Wino Woody not only won in most of the pickle competitions but also cleaned up in corn relish and piccalilli. Only his champagne jelly seems to fail at the fair. Following one triumph at the Los Angeles fair, Woody sounded off to a Los Angeles *Times* reporter who wrote: "Modest Woody attributes his success in being a big winner for 23 straight years in the foods division of the Los Angeles County Fair to the honesty and integrity of California judges, all sweet and charming ladies. He won't say the Texas judges at Terlingua are dishonest but there might be a wee bit of prejudice against a man known worldwide for his culinary skills who is from the nation's largest state in population." The truth is there have been several judges from California each time Woody has competed at Terlingua.

Mr. De Silva prepares his chili in a half-moon-shaped Oriental cooking pot called a wok.

One of his statements before the tournament in 1968 was that "Fowler will be easy to defeat if my wok works. I'm having trouble finding a burner big enough to thoroughly heat the base of my wok, which has a very broad bottom like Wick Fowler."

Also Woody had his assistant, Ormly Gumfudgin!, passing out newspaper clippings showing that Mr. De Silva had taken first prize in pickles for all those years at the Los Angeles County Fair.

Mr. De Silva's "wok troubles" were solved in Terlingua when he was loaned a huge, sixty-thousand-BTU gas burner by Archie Francis of Tyler, Texas, a gas burner with enough area to heat evenly the gargantuan Chinese cooking pot.

"Now I will carry California and Cucamonga to glory!" Wino Woody predicted before doing battle with Fowler.

It didn't work out quite that way.

I thought H. Allen Smith was at home on his mountaintop above Alpine treating his hives during the '68 cookoff. Anyway, he made an erroneous report on the event, especially with regard to Wino Woody's behavior patterns during the contest. Now Mr. De Silva is a good clown, a biscuit-bodied little man with a red radish of a nose, and he *is* much given to drink.

Smith suggested Woody was downright intoxicated during the duel with Fowler: "He [Wino Woody] fell off the platform three times before he got on it. He made a brief speech nominating Harold Stassen for President and thanked the people of Philadelphia for being so kind to him . . ."

At least Mr. De Silva was sober enough to confide to me up there on the saloon veranda that one of the secret ingredients for the alleged fine flavor of his chili (besides using champagne to marinate the meat and to thin the broth) was a spice called "woodruff," defined in Webster as a "low, aromatic, rubiaceous herb."

Mr. De Silva did have difficulty with the big burner under the wok. His clothing was more or less saturated with champagne and he set himself afire. After the flames were put out on his clothing, he caused the fire to spread when he tried to douse some flames on the table under his burner by spraying them with champagne.

Fowler's chili was vastly superior to his opponent's, just as it had been against Soupy Smith the year before.

Yet Wick wasn't destined to win in '68. Somehow the judging panel wound up with a majority of Wino Woody's buddies from California, including the sports car designer and auto racer Carroll Shelby and the former astronaut Scott Carpenter.

De Silva would probably have won an undeserved title if there hadn't been a tawdry drama at the end of the contest, dreamed up by some press agents who'd seen too many wrestling matches. The judges had written out their votes and put them in a ballot box. Masked men, carrying firearms, appeared and took the ballot box and threw it into one of the restrooms over a mine shaft. By this time the California judges were too far gone in champagne for decisiveness. And the referee had to declare another draw.

In 1969 the cookoff at Terlingua ceased to be a *mano a mano* affair.

In the '69 cookoff Wick Fowler and Woodruff De Silva returned, although Wino Woody barely made it. And a pair of interesting new personalities competed in the tournament for the first time: Joe DeFrates, the Illinois chili king, and C. V. Wood, Jr., president of the McCulloch Corporation (oil, chain saws, resort cities, etc.), a native of Amarillo, Texas, who lived in California and Arizona.

DeFrates is an inhabitant of Springfield, the Illinois capital which also claims to the "The Chilli [sic] Capital of the World."

Joe DeFrates said that his father, the late Walter (Port) DeFrates, learned to make good Texas-style chili in the years just before World War I while working as a bartender in a Dallas saloon. The saloon served chili as part of its free lunch.

Port DeFrates returned to his native Springfield and started the chili canning factory which his sons have continued to operate, called "The Chilli Man," for they seem to spell chili with an extra "l" in Illinois. Port DeFrates' brother, the late Ray DeFrates, established another Springfield chili cannery, "Ray's Brand," which is still a successful business.

Springfield did seem to have more chili parlors than any other American city in the 1970s. Leafing through the *Illinois State Journal*, the local daily, you find dozens of advertisements of cafés and taverns which serve "chilli," such as a chain called the Chilli Den Parlors, the Jailhouse Tavern, The Cozy Drive-in ("The same chilli recipe for 27 years"), Herron's ("Serving the best chilli for 24 years"), Tom Thumb ("Try our delicious greaseless chilli"), Norby Andy ("If you're looking for a chilli to tantalize the proboscis"), and even the Ann Rutledge Pancake House in Lincoln Center ("Chilli as it should be made").

One tavern advertises "chilli and go-go-girls."

"Springfield folks are mad about chilli," said Joe DeFrates. "We almost certainly have more regular chilli eaters than any other city on earth. And to think that this miserable, flea-bitten ghost town, Terlingua, should try to usurp Springfield's title as the Chilli Capital of the World."

DeFrates is one of the most pleasing personalities to appear at Terlingua, a great chili, or chilli, ambassador for his state.

C. V. Wood was known internationally as the guy who bought London Bridge, tore it down, and moved all the pieces to the Arizona desert where it was reassembled at Lake Havasu City. There the McCulloch Corporation has built one of its many resort cities. C.V. is also one of the most dedicated of chili heads. For example, his breakfast when he's at home is usually a bowl of chili con carne of his own concoction — and a Pepsi.

He took a cupboard of herbs and other spices and some rather mysterious ingredients on each of his trips to Terlingua. And he claims that his "secret chili recipe," which includes green chilies and, incredibly, lime juice, takes at least a thousand words to describe.

Wood attended several Texas colleges and then wound up taking an engineering degree at Oklahoma University. At twenty-eight he was chief industrial engineer for Convair, a San Diego division of General Dynamics. He was in on the design and was the first general manager of Disneyland. He joined McCulloch in 1961, and a Los Angeles *Times* business writer says he is "respected as a tough competitor and a shrewd money manager."

I believe that Wick Fowler is the world's greatest chili cook. Yet Wickford lost again in the curious 1969 tournament at Terlingua.

C. V. Wood won. I was the referee, and I believe that *most* of those on the judges' panel were honest. I say *most*. H. Allen Smith was permitted to be a judge, and I must say his behavior on the '69 panel was highly suspicious. He later confessed in a magazine article: "I approached him [C. V. Wood] on the platform when he was cooking in 1969. Being a judge in that contest, I spoke pleasantly, hoping for a bribe, and he snarled: 'Get away, boy, you bother me.' He was cooking a concoction called 'green chili' which an hour or so later brought him the title. It looked ghastly . . ."

After failing to get a bribe from Wood, Judge Smith turned his attention to Joe DeFrates. Fowler interrupted his cooking to protest that Smith was whispering to the Illinois champion, which he called "unseeming judicial behavior." Sure enough Smith voted DeFrates for first place with this curious explanation: "I'm not voting for his chili. I'm voting because DeFrates comes from Illinois, and that's where I was born."

It may have been that, as referee, I permitted too many Californians on the judging panel, and the non-California judges may have been influenced by C. V. Wood's cheering section, a committee of beautiful girls, some of them starlets, whom he brought from California in his personal jet aircraft.

Anyway, Wood and his green chili won the '69 championship with Fowler an angry second and DeFrates in third place.

Poor Woody De Silva had trouble all the way. He was such a shoo-in for the annual championship in California that not many chili heads had bothered to attend the contest, which tried to lure spectators with this teaser, "See lovely Swedish girls chop up onions."

Wino Woody had a disastrous trip from his home in Cucamonga to the 1969 cookoff. He arrived late and reported that he "got lost" on the way in El Paso, in Juárez, Mexico, and even in Terlingua's neighboring hamlet, Study Butte.

Then Woody marinated his beef so generously with champagne that the chili he finally produced must have been 12 percent alcohol, and not nearly up to normal standard for a De Silva pot. Also he had the wok down on the veranda porch once and fell in his chili, which made the judges queasy about tasting it.

Some of the delegates from afar had even more troubles than Mr. De Silva in finding Terlingua for the '69 cookoff. A big planeload of rooters from Springfield, Illinois, came to back Joe DeFrates. Only when they arrived it was just being announced that Joe had finished a hot third. And the Springfield fans also were witnesses to the spectacle of Wick Fowler throwing a temper tantrum over taking second place to Wood. (Wick hurled the chamber-pot trophy he was awarded against an adobe wall, probably destroying its usefulness.)

The airplane from Springfield had navigation problems and its first landing was in Mexico.

There was some vulgar boasting in Arizona and California after C. V. Wood won his first world championship.

I was used to ridicule from Arizona pundits. For example, a Phoenix newspaper columnist, Bert Fireman, once made the claim that Texas has an unusual number of left-handed school children "all using their little southpaws to spoon up greasy Texas chili." And another former Phoenix columnist, Don Dedara, declared: "If ever a barge full of Texas chili runs aground off Corpus Christi, no amount of detergent will clean up the scum on the Gulf of Mexico beaches . . ."

Either C. V. Wood or his supporters had the audacity to buy a full page advertisement in the November 7, 1969, issue of the Los Angeles *Times* which read in part:

"Your [Mr. Wood's] achievement in winning the 1969 World Championship Chili Cookoff at Terlingua, Texas, is a significant milestone in the relentless advancement of the art of chili preparation. We especially honor your [Mr. Wood's] courage in challenging the orthodox methods and product of the traditional red school of chili con carne. We therefore feel it appropriate to salute the integrity and fairness of the judges, Carroll Shelby, H. Allen Smith, Hamilton Rial, Mayor Dave Witts of Terlingua, Tom Hill, and Frank Tolbert."

11. Honest Judging at Last

". . . a dog-eared sultan riding in a double-decker London bus with a gaggle of shapely girls . . ."

Smith, on Wood

The first two cookoffs had been pretty much spoofs. In the '69 affair the judges, except for Smith, were honest, but they may have been influenced by Wood's starlets brushing up against them.

Anyway, the 1970 World Series saw the dawn of an era of honest judging at Terlingua. To keep down complaints from losing contestants, Referee Tolbert secured the services on the judges' panel in '70 and '71 of the international renowned mentalist Peter Hurkos. He is the clairvoyant who was used by police departments in several murder cases, including the ones involving the Boston Strangler and Sharon Tate. My thinking was that the contestants would feel better if the celebrated "mind reader" were on the panel, where he could sense if any of the judges were crooked.

Anyway, in 1970 at Terlingua, Wick Fowler finally won the world championship he had so long deserved. Unexpectedly, his greatest competition came from a tall Indian in buckskins, feathers, and beads, Fulton Battise, principal chief of the Alabama-Coushatta tribes, whose reservation is in beautiful high pines country in East Texas.

Defending Champion C. V. Wood arrived for the 1970 cookoff with a court including a half-dozen Hollywood actresses and models and forty or fifty other assorted California and Arizona characters. They came in Mr. Wood's jet plane and in a big, four-motored prop plane fitted out grandly as a drawing room, the two aircraft landing at Fritz Kahl's Marfa airport, that being the only strip in the Big Bend which would accommodate them.

Mr. Wood's personal Dixieland band played during the disembarkation. It's around 120 miles from Marfa to Terlingua. Wood's entourage was transported to the cookoff scene in a bunch of rented cars, although C.V. didn't go all the way in a passenger car. The last few miles to Terlingua, Wood and the girls and the bandsmen rode in a double-decker London city bus, C.V. wearing a crown of red chili peppers and furry monarchial robes.

Referee Tolbert let H. Allen Smith be a judge again, although Smith admitted in an article in the Chicago *Tribune* that an "Election Reform Committee has been set up to look into the 'odd' judging standards at Terlingua. It is my feeling that his nefarious probe is directed in the main at me."

Smith was right. I'd warned him about soliciting bribes from contestants.

H. Allen still held a grudge against C. V. Wood, writing what sounded to me in part like a quotation from Sam Goldwyn that "in 1969 a man named C. V. Wood, Jr., came out of the West and captured the championship in a frightful carriage of misjustice."

Smith turned his spite on Mr. Wood by writing in the Chicago *Tribune:* "He [C.V.] turned up at the 1970 fiesta dressed as some kind of dog-eared sultan and riding in a double-decker London bus with a gaggle of shapely California girls . . . (Then) Wood did not cook and he would give no reason for his withdrawl. I think he brought no chili pot to the tournament because he had been held up to almost universal scorn and ridicule . . ."

The truth is that C.V. was a little worn out from wearing all those robes and the kingly crown and from overacting in his role as defending world champion. And he asked Referee Tolbert if he could sit this one out and come back and really cook next year.

He sat on a throne he'd fetched along in his jet, and watched the proceedings.

Wick Fowler arrived a little late because he'd had trouble working his Cadillac through a broken field of campers and motor homes parked around the Chisos Oasis gallery. And the spectators were estimated at five thousand.

Once he got started, Mr. Fowler composed a poem of a chili pot, possibly the best in the history of the World Series.

Indian Chief Fulton Battise is recognized as the leading chef on his reservation. It was only about a month before, however, that he'd started making chili, using the standard Texas-style chili recipe in this book.

Chief Battise finished second and might have given Fowler more trouble if the Indian executive's concoction, made with big chunks of beef, hadn't contained a little too much grease and chili peppers for the delicate taste buds of certain of the judges from California and Illinois.

As usual, H. Allen Smith made a mockery of his judicial duties. He refused to taste from any pot except that of Illinois champion Joe DeFrates, and he got in a big row with several of the "outlaw" women cooks whom the referee had permitted to compete.

As usual, Joe DeFrates won the popularity contest with the crowd and finished a deserved third. The Illinois entry did this in spite of the fact that the crowd once broke through the gallery and in clamoring for samples of his chili con carne y frijoles almost knocked the DeFrates pot off the stove before it had been judged.

Chalio Salis, the Mexican champion from Durango, spent most of his time at this fourth cookoff trying to ingratiate himself with the judges by whipping out his guitar and singing border ballads in a pleasing baritone. Most of his cooking was done by his decorative helper, a Mexican blonde. Chalio's chili was too heavily laced with furies and some other fierce peppers for the Yankee types among the judges to give him many points.

Hard-luck champion of the fourth series was the Arkansas champion, Dick Wilcox of Fort Smith. Like most of the contestants, Mr. Wilcox and his good-looking young wife had spent the night at El Paisano Hotel in Marfa, about a hundred air miles north of Terlingua. When the Arkansas chili king set up to cook on the Chisos Oasis gallery, he discovered he'd left his pot and other vital equipment back in Marfa.

Dick had to hire a light plane to go back to Marfa and get his cooking equipment. And when he returned he had to perform hurriedly and the result was nothing like his usual excellent pot of chili, according to his Arkansas supporters.

At the 1970 cookoff there were three attractive yet un-invited women contestants, Janice Constantine of Midland, Pat Beck of Odessa, and Amber Cree of Abilene.

Janice Constantine tried to influence the judges with a mini-mini costume. She arrived in a chauffeured Rolls Royce with a "social secretary" and servants who set up a silver table service with live music furnished by the first violinist of the Midland-Odessa Symphony Orchestra, the musician in for-mal evening attire. Janice is said to be one of the best all-around cooks in Midland. Her chili, however, was rated poorly by the judges, including the only woman on the panel, actress Ruta Lee of Los Angeles.

Amber Cree, a very good-looking woman, had a male helper she declared to be an Arabian. He was done up in a burnoose and hood and chanted what seemed to be gibberish as he stirred his chili pot, while Amber stood around and looked coolly beautiful. The result in the pot was rated poorly.

Referee Tolbert had permitted the women to compete because he feared that otherwise the two thousand or more women in the crowd might riot.

There has never been any prejudice against women cooks at Terlingua except in the case of H. Allen Smith when he has been suffered to be a judge.

Jerry Fales, a New York City magazine editor, won the New York state championship in '69, '70, and '71, and I encouraged her to come to Terlingua each time, only she said she couldn't spare the time from her editorial and housewifely duties.

Yet a contestant must have finished at least third in an authorized state chili cookoff or in one sponsored by an Indian nation to be eligible at Terlingua. This is the only requirement.

H. Allen Smith is the only cookoff judge who has been opposed to permitting women in the World Series. He once wrote: "No woman should be allowed near an iron chili pot . . . chili is a man's dish and should be cooked only by male humanoids . . ."

Soupy Smith used his influence in Alpine to get an order at the Brewster County courthouse for the arrest of poor Janice Constantine.

While Janice *was* making something of a pest of herself, the rest of us thought Smith was behaving rather churlishly in having the woman arrested on a charge of "trying to cook chili while then and there being a female person."

Wick Fowler and C. V. Wood both began to suffer from the grandeur syndrome; at least that's my analysis of why they demanded that Referee Tolbert let them compete *mano a mano* in a "Super Bowl" at the 1971 Terlingua tournament.

The other state champions would vie for a more plain-vanilla version of the world championship. The winner among the state champions would earn the right to meet the victor of the Wood-Fowler duel in a 1972 "Super Bowl."

"Wick is the only person in the world capable of competing with me," said Mr. Wood. Fowler said he was interested in revenge for Wood's beating him in '69 and "chickening out"in '70. Also, Wickford said he was tired of competing against "peasants such as Smith and Wino Woody."

The referee of the Terlingua contests had been adversely criticized by many for permitting Fowler automatically to represent the State of Texas in the World Series. So in 1970 the first Texas cookoff was held at San Marcos, Texas, on the grounds of the Aquarena resort at the headwaters of the San Marcos River. The '71 state cookoff was enacted at San Marcos also.

I had no control over the San Marcos rules, though, and was an innocent victim of many protests when women were excluded from the state cookoff. Harold Robbins, one of the fellows who run the San Marcos contests, is of the H. Allen school of thought on women and chili.

"No women is qualified to cook chili," Mr. Robbins declared flatly in a newspaper interview.

Sam Kindrick, a columnist for the San Antonio *Express*, backed Mr. Robbins, writing: "The female militants trying to crash the chili cookoff for men only at San Marcos are a bunch of a little old ladies in tennis shoes."

The resulting female anger caused Mrs. Mickey Trent and other female chili heads of the state to organize the Hell Hath No Fury Chili Society. And the Dallas-based society began to make plans for a state cookoff after I told them that the winner, second finisher, and third would be permitted to vie for the title at Terlingua.

Alex Burton, an electronic journalist who had suggested the name of the Hell Hath No, etc., Society, also believed that good sites for the "cook-in" (that's what the women persisted in styling it) would be the Texas towns of either Hearne or Lovelady. Mrs. Trent wrote to the chambers of commerce of Hearne and Lovelady and received no reply.

Finally, I talked Hondo Crouch and Guich Koock into providing the site. Hondo and Guich are co-owners of the entire business section of the village of Luckenbach in the Texas hill country. And this hamlet — with its ramshackle general store and tavern originally an Indian trading post — hasn't changed much since it was settled by colonists from Germany around 1850.

A blue-eyed, very blond San Antonio housewife, Cindi Craig, won the women's title at Luckenbach — it was called the first annual Susan B. Anthony Memorial Cook-in.

Cindi's recipe was certainly unique, calling for in addition to 7 cups of lean chuck roast beef chopped to bite size, 18 skinless German-style smoked sausage links, and almost 2 cans of beer (she specified Pearl).

Second place went to an extremely decorative Houston woman, Allegheny Janie Schofield, who wore hot pants and sweater and nothing much else. Mrs. Leola Branch, also of Houston, a charming black woman, tied for third with a large committee (too many to recite here) of the University of Texas students all working over one pot. (Teams aren't allowed in the World Series at Terlingua.)

After the cook-in, there was a dance in Luckenbach's nineteenth-century dance hall/theater-in-the-round, with music furnished by Uncle Felix Pehl and his oompah band from nearby Luckenbach. The first Texas women's chili bust was quite a success.

To illustrate the sort of inaccurate reporting that comes out of Terlingua, a Britisher, Peter Moseley, representing the Reuter's News Agency at the '71 World Series, supplied this misinformation:

"The all-male team of judges at the 5th Annual World Chili Cookoff disqualified all the women contestants on the grounds they submitted their entries thirty seconds too late."

There was no truth to this. The only one disqualified was the ubiquitous Janice Constantine. She had declined to take her chances in the women's cook-in at Luckenbach, so she just flat wasn't eligible. Early on the November morn of the '71 cookoff, her servants appeared and raised a marquee under which Janice was to cook squarely in front of the veranda which serves both the saloon and the old opera house, now only four roofless adobe walls. I had Janice's stooges pick up the canopy and move it out in the cactus flats near the Terlingua jail.

The 1971 panel certainly wasn't all-male. Peter Moseley ignored the fact that there were three actresses from California among the judges, Joanne Dru, Ruta Lee, and Sue Oliver. Also, H. Allen Smith, with his bitter prejudice against women chili cooks, had come down with another case of the hives and wasn't on the judges' panel this time. And don't forget that mentalist Peter Hurkos was back to ensure that the judges' thoughts were pure.

Peter Moseley's article for Reuter's was mostly about La Constantine: "Under an elegant canopy, amid the cactus and tumbleweed, a violinist in full concert gear played softly as the clientele sampled Miss Janice Constantine's chili from silver salvers.

"Miss Janice's butler, social secretary, and press secretary stood in attendance while her chauffeur kept an anxious eye on the Rolls Royce, the car surrounded by curious cowboys.

"Janice Constantine herself, of Midland, Texas, the 'disputed queen of the chili world,' reigned graciously over the scene in royal regalia of crown, scepter, and hot pants. Along with a lady named Allegheny Janie Schofield and three or four other brave members of the 'Hell Hath No Fury Chili Society,' Miss Janice was making yet another bid to break the male stranglehold on the international chili contest. They failed."

Peter Moseley ignored or didn't know that Joyce Newlin finished third in the competition among the state champions.

She was chosen to cook for the team of University of Texas coeds who'd also tied for third at Luckenbach.

Not even Janice Constantine could compete with some of the men in the matter of spectacular entourages.

The Tigua Indians from El Paso were there in colorful costumes of their pueblo days to support their tribal champion, Jose Sierra (Joe Mountain). The Tiguas beat on their sacred three-hundred-year-old ceremonial drum (a musical instrument which they claim has "sex") and danced while Joe Sierra first put thick-meated, shoulderless chili pepper pods in a huge pot about a third of the way up and then added the other ingredients.

As the powerful chili simmered, the Tiguas sniffed the peppery aromas and expressed their pleasure by stopping dancing long enough to fire ten-gauge shotguns into the air.

Fulton Battise, the Alabama-Coushatta tribes' principal chief, brought along his medicine man, Lester Battise, a 250-pounder whose attire included a buffalo scalp hat with horns, and some "no rain dancers."

There's never been even a threat of rain at any of the chili cookoffs. But in the 1971 Texas cookoff for men only at San Marcos, rains began to fall about the time the contestants had their pots simmering under the dark sky. Rain would have been a disaster, especially for those such as Chief Battise, who were using wood fires. Medicine Man Lester Battise, looking fierce under his horned scalp hat and with a huge drum riding against his broad midriff, announced to the crowd:

"Many times I have beaten this drum while our girls and boys did rain dances. Now we will attempt an '*ooh-eeh-bah-bitly*' or 'no rain dance'." The Indians put on a humdinger of an ooh-eeh-bah-bitly, for they'd no more finished than the rains stopped, and there were only a few sprinkles for the rest of the contest. Chief Battise won the state championship at San Marcos that day.

At Terlingua during the '71 cookoff the Tiguas and the Alabama-Coushattas were also having a sort of informal bread-making battle.

The Tiguas arrived the night before and raised an adobe oven in which they composed tasty unleavened bread with greasewood as the fuel.

At the same time, the Alabama-Coushatta women were busy making a delicious version of squaw bread. These Indian breads served the judges well to cool off their mouths between spoonfuls of chili.

Because I'd permitted so many Indians to enter, the defending champion, Wick Fowler, decided to come dressed as General George Armstrong Custer, with a blue cavalry outfit over his 250-pound figure, and wearing a scraggly yellow wig under his campaign hat.

Joe DeFrates wore a Lincolnesque stovepipe hat in the Springfield, Illinois, motif. On the way to the '71 Terlingua cookoff, Mr. DeFrates had to change planes in Dallas, and before getting off at Dallas he absentmindedly left his stovepipe hat on the aircraft. While wandering around in the Dallas airport lobby, DeFrates came face to face with a stranger wearing an Abe Lincoln hat. "I thought at first that these hats must be becoming fashionable outside of Springfield," said Joe. "Then I realized this guy was wearing *my* hat. The stranger said he'd just picked it up when he got off the airplane from Springfield, thinking it was some kind of souvenir. He gave me my hat without an argument."

As usual the New York champion, Jerry Fales, informed me that she couldn't get away from her job on the magazine, and anyway she wasn't too keen on cooking from scratch in the eighty-degree heat and uproar of the ghost town.

Fortunately, there was George Wright to represent New York State.

George Wright is the chili chef for Clint Murchison, Jr.'s Dallas Cowboy Restaurant on Forty-ninth Street near Park Avenue in New York City. The accent is on Texas-style chili, of which the Dallas Cowboy serves the best in New York or on the whole Eastern seaboard.

George Wright is a busy man. It takes around three tons of chili a week for the Dallas Cowboy's customers. However, at the time of the 1971 New York State chili cookoff, in an apartment complex on East Eighty-eighth Street, the Dallas Cowboy Restaurant had not been opened and George Wright was still in Dallas when I informed him that the New York tournament was the following day. He flew to New York, spent hours and no telling how much cab fare going around Manhattan trying to get the proper ingredients. He got to the cookoff barely on time and finished second, back of the defending New York champion, Mrs. Jerry Fales.

Perhaps influenced by Janice Constantine's violinist, George Wright decided that since he was representing sophisticated Manhattan it would be good showmanship to cook at Terlingua in a full dress suit and silk top hat.

So he rented one. The New York rental clerk was curious: "I suppose you'll wear this suit and topper to some grand occasion, sir?"

"Sure," replied Mr. Wright. "I'm going to wear it to cook chili in a ghost town on the Rio Grande."

C. V. Wood, Jr. claimed he was cooking green pepper chili in the '71 Super Bowl. And yet his chili was fully as red as Fowler's orthodox Texas-style chili.

I thought I'd devised a protest-proof judging system for the duel between these two hard losers. The judges were back in the ruins of the opera house, away from the influence of the contestants and the crowd and Wood's cheerleaders.

Back in the opera house the judges were served bowls of both Fowler's and Wood's chili, identifiable as far as I could see only by different styles of spoons. And the judges didn't know about those spoons. Only the referee knew.

The judges picked Wood the winner. This surprised me. For when Smith had to bow out the majority of the judges were Texans. Yet it was an honest decision.

Fowler didn't think so. He claimed that the judges didn't even taste his chili, although I'd seen to it that several bowls of his produce had been convoyed back into the opera house ruins. And all the judges durned sure tasted the chili of both of the Super Bowl gladiators.

The wire services were as usual somewhat inaccurate. One said that the angry Fowler chased the judges across Dirty Woman Creek. Not so. Fowler just jumped up and down a lot on the veranda while cussing the judges.

C. V. Wood had earlier difficulties. He was supposed to have arrived in Terlingua in a seventy-thousand-cubic-foot-capacity hot air balloon. But his henchmen couldn't get it inflated in time. Later they got the balloon up above the crowd in the ghost town (estimated at between five thousand and eight thousand), but for some reason the balloon suddenly collapsed on people and motor vehicles. There was no damage except to Wood's feelings. He had his heart set on arriving at Terlingua in the gondola of a giant balloon.

Wood was in a bad mood during the cooking, but when it was announced he'd won he put on his crown and robes and started being quite immodest, and in fact accused Fowler of using "commercially prepared ingredients which I never do, any more than I'd prefer a paint-by-the-numbers-kit painting over one by Picasso." (Fowler does manufacture packaged ingredients for making chili, but he cooks strictly from scratch at Terlingua.)

A youthful visitor from Los Angeles said to me: "You know the best thing about this event? No pigs! That's the best thing." He added: "It's really wonderful to see thousands of people from all over the nation assemble in this ghost town and nothing rough happens, and yet you have no policemen standing around."

As far as I know there were no policemen on duty in the blessed sweet desert air at the '71 cookoff, or at any previous one. That is, if you don't count the harried Department of Public Safety men (state troopers) who were on the roads to

Terlingua trying to straighten out the traffic problems.

When it came time to judge the tournament of the state champions, two on the panel, Sue Oliver, the lovely young actress, and the former astronaut Scott Carpenter got lost in the crowd, and I could have used some policemen to try and find the missing judges and to escort the remaining judges through the throng.

When the veranda became too crowded earlier in the day, I'd had some of the state champions do their cooking down among the spectators. Some were down there by choice, such as the Tigua Indians who wanted to be next to their adobe oven and wished open space for drumming and dancing. (They created even more dancing space in the crowd when they started firing those ten-gauge shotguns into the air.)

I wasn't a judge in '71. Yet to my taste the best chili in that cookoff came from the pot of the New York champion, George Wright. His Terlingua chili had more authority, pepper-wise, than what he serves in Manhattan, yet it wasn't so heavily charged as to discourage the more tender palates, including those of the California actresses serving as judges, Mr. Wright's chili was an almost unanimous choice for first place among the state champions, I was told later by the judge I use to keep score (in Spanish), Enrique Vásquez, a Uvalde restaurateur who affects unique headgear such as a hat made of an armadillo shell.

His Illinois compadre wasn't around to judge. Still Joe DeFrates easily won second. And, as recited earlier in this narrative, Joyce Newlin, the Hell Hath No Fury Society entry, finished third. The University of Texas coed became the first girl-type to win something at Terlingua.

Janice Constantine put on her crown and crowded in to pose with the winners during picture-taking time.

One of the wire service reports, written by a New Yorker, said that the '71 cookoff signified the "decline" of Texas-style chili "since both major championships were won by either an Arizona inhabitant or a New Yorker." As mentioned before here, C. V. Wood was born and raised in Amarillo, and Wright is from Henderson in East Texas.

C.V. didn't waste any time in Terlingua after winning the Super Bowl. He gathered up his deflated balloon, his girl cheerleaders, his Las Vegas line of dancing girls, his bandsmen, and headed for the airport at Marfa.

The year 1971 was not a good one for Wick Fowler. He had been defeated in a race for city councilman of Austin, Texas, leading in the primary and then losing narrowly in a runoff in which his wife, Bess, was campaigning against him. Mrs. Fowler wanted Wickford to stay out of politics.

I noticed that both the Alabama-Coushatta and Tigua Indians were very careful to put out their mesquite or greasewood fires before they left, the Tiguas heading upriver for dinner at a restaurant and cabaret in Ojinaga, the Mexican city across the Rio Bravo from Presidio, Texas. And in the cabaret even the eighty-year-old cacique of the tribe, Jose Granillo, went in for a lot of ballroom dancing. The Alabama-Coushattas are more Calvinistic types, and they simply packed up and headed back on the eight-hundred-mile journey to their domain in East Texas' Big Thicket (a jungle of high pines and hardwoods, with many magnolias and palmetto plantations).

After posing with the winners for the television and wire service photographers, Janice Constantine had her servants fold her marquee and pack the silver and napery, and then Janice and her court, including the fiddler in evening clothes, took off in the Rolls Royce.

After he won the title, George stayed around talking to people in the ghost town until after sundown. Then he packed up his cooking gear and took off in his rented car.

Somehow Mr. Wright took the wrong road and wound up still on pavement but on a side road in the desert darkness. Without even hitting an obstacle one wheel came off the rented car. Wright was driving slowly and wasn't hurt.

He didn't know what else to do, so he locked up the car and started hiking up the lonely road, still wearing his full dress suit and silk top hat.

A pickup truck came up over a rise in the road and caught the formally attired pedestrian in the headlights.

The driver first backed up. Apparently, he couldn't quite believe what he saw in the ranch road. Then the pickup truck driver turned his machine off in the pasture and studied George in his headlights at a new angle.

Finally, the truck was propelled back on the road fairly close to George. An old rancher, who it turned out didn't know anything about the chili cookoff, stuck his head out of one side of the truck and yelled: "Who and what in the hell are you?"

George convinced the cowman he was harmless. And the new champion, in silk hat and tails, hitched a ride in to Alpine.

12. Drugstore Chili
and Other Extraordinaries

"You can settle in a Terlingua restroom, cup an ear, and hear community singing in China."

Comment on the facilities
built over open mine shafts

Joe Sierra, chief chili maker for the Tigua Indians of El Paso, was quite unhappy when his composition, containing about a third of a pot of fiery anchos and other muscular chili peppers, didn't do well in the judging at Terlingua. In fact, one of the actress-judges from California said she feared that one more taste of Tigua chili and her mouth would be permanently damaged.

"What these *lafas* want, drugstore chili?" Joe Sierra asked, *lafa* being an abbreviation of the agglutinative definition for a white person in the Tigua (pronounced "tee-wah") language.

Margaret Cousins, a chili authority mentioned previously in this book, would never agree with Joe Sierra that drugstore chili was so bad — at least in the days when Maggie

Cousins was a kid in Texas.

Maggie Cousins once wrote a nostalgic essay on the subject of Drugstore Chili:

"In their books on chili, Frank Tolbert and H. Allen Smith have praised certain varieties of chili con carne. Jail House Chili has received special praise from Tolbert, as apparently the chili produced in county lockups in the Southwest has a very special haute cuisine quality.

"As I have never been in jail, I have not sampled this gourmet treat, yet it might be worth an infringement of the law.

"Nobody has said anything about Drugstore Chili. So I wish to lay my little laurel wreath on this pot. Some of the great chili memories of my rich, full life are concerned with Drugstore Chili.

"My father (a drugstore owner) did not think much of chili in a drug store, feeling the odor of garlic did not mix suitably with the fragrance that belonged properly to drug stores, but this never deterred me from the counters of his competitors.

"Drugstore Chili, albeit a plebeian stew, had a very special evanescence and was always full of beans. Also nobody stopped you from crumbling the saltines into it the way they did at home.

"It was served in a large white crockery bowl with a plate of crackers, all you could eat for fifteen cents. I don't know what the drugstore cooks put in it but it was habit forming."

Because we lured him to the Big Bend country to cook in the first World Series, Tom Tierney and Tolbert are blamed for H. Allen Smith's moving to Alpine, the nearest town of any size to Terlingua.

H.A. found the climate of the West Texas mountains so kind that he left Mount Kisco, New York (some say about two hundred yards ahead of a posse), and built a nine-thousand-dollar shrine for dwelling on a mountain overlooking Alpine, and settled into being the resident curmudgeon.

Soon after becoming an Alpine inhabitant, Soupy Smith began saying some very churlish things in national and local prints and even on a national television show. He even declared that many Alpine citizens, through some biological miracle, are of canine descent on the maternal side. Only he wasn't that subtle in his phraseology. And many of the big Bend burghers have complained to Tolbert that I should bear primal guilt for the Smithsonian presence in Alpine.

Smith claimed he left Mount Kisco to get away from hippies and pollution. He described Alpine at first in a kindly way as "a town of under 6,000 souls . . . 4,500 feet above sea level and surrounded by fairly spectacular mountain peaks. It is a town awash with strong characters . . . The principal industry (next to God) is a university (Sul Ross State) with an enrollment of about 2,000 . . . Fred Allen once described me as 'The Screwballs' Boswell.' So now I've discovered a gold mine. I can make a living for the rest of my life writing about the lunatic fringe in Alpine, Texas. If none of the worms and weirdos move away."

I caught some complaints from Smith's late-blooming book on chili. For instance, a woman from Pasadena, Texas, wrote me: "I made some chili from a recipe on page 72 of the first edition of H. Allen Smith's book on chili. This recipe calls for 3 pounds of lean meat and 10 cloves of garlic, among other ingredients. Well, I followed the instructions faithfully and those 10 cloves of garlic really stunk up my kitchen. Also my husband cussed after only one taste of the Smith-style chili and refused to eat any more."

The Los Angeles *Times'* Sunday magazine, called *West*, published an insulting and inaccurate report on the 1970 cookoff at Terlingua. The author was one Burt Prelutsky, and he got off to a bad start with "in case Terlingua doesn't ring any bells it's because the place is a ghost town. The only time it has a population consisting of anything besides rattlesnakes and jackrabbits is the day of the annual cookout.

"The audience arrived by aircraft, cars, trailers, and in two instances by parachutes. (Wrong, Mr. Prelutsky, three fellows dropped in on the World Series by parachutes.)

"Why they come to Terlingua is a little harder to determine. There's no water, no electricity, no toilets. The nearest motel is 300 miles away. They stand out there in the sun for six hours just watching chili being cooked . . ."

To start with, Terlingua has water; the spring-fed, ever-flowing stream called Terlingua Creek and its intermittently wet satellite, Dirty Woman Creek.

The Terlingua saloon, called the Chisos Oasis, has electrical connections. And as to Bungler Prelutsky's charge that there are no toilets, there are six restrooms — all over open mine shafts. In fact, Terlingua has probably the world's deepest restrooms, and someone said: "You can settle in a Terlingua restroom, cup an ear, and hear community singing in China."

Terlingua also has a motel, called Casa Del Mina, or House of the Mine. And there are other, lesser motels in the village of Study Butte, a few miles down the road; and a luxurious motel and complex of cabins in The Basin of the Chisos Mountains, only about a thirty-five-mile, uphill drive from Terlingua; and, of course, several first-class motels in Alpine, eighty miles to the north.

13. Tamales and Enchiladas

"They ain't but two people on earth who can make a real tamale, and I'm both of them."

Early Caldwell,
The World's Greatest Tamale King

Early Caldwell, a tall, elderly Negro from Athens, Texas, who has been composing superlative hot tamales for more than fifty years, told me as he worked over a wood cooking stove full of blackjack oak coals:

"I make what I call a Western Union tamale. You know what a Western Union tamale is? You cook it here in Athens and you can smell it away off in Dallas. You can't make a Western Union tamale except over a wood stove."

Early Caldwell, a man of good countenance and quaint, wise speech habits, bills himself "The World's Greatest Tamale King" on the calendars he sends to friends and clients.

Athens is said to have produced more multimillionaires than any other town of its size in the nation. Clint Murchison, Sr. and the late "billionaire bachelor," Sid Richardson, are conspicuous examples.

"Mr. Clint Murchison, Mr. Sid Richardson, and Mr. Arch Underwood, and such-like gentlemen was my boyhood friends here in Athens," he said. "We used to go swimming down near the brickyard. And they is all twenty-cent customers of mine."

By "twenty-cent customers," Caldwell means those clients who have been buying tamales from him since the long-ago days when he charged only twenty cents a dozen for tamales made just as uncompromisingly well as those for which he gets seventy-five cents a dozen today.

In Athens, the corner near the square at 201 East Tyler Street in called "Early's Corner." For three days each week almost every week since 1919, Caldwell has appeared on that corner to sell his delicious wares. He parks his car at the corner and it's not long before he has sold all the tamales he has in stock. When the town put in parking meters in the downtown section, the mayor at the time told Early: "Unless the public starts raising sand about it, you don't have to put any coins in the meter on your corner." No one raised any sand.

Early spends most of one day making tamales over the wood stove in his clean little kitchen. Like the true artist he is, he won't change his "making" and "selling" days for business reasons. To illustrate this, on a certain Friday several years ago there were thousands of people in Athens for the annual Old Fiddlers' Contests. Yet Early sold no tamales on the corner that day. For Friday was a "making" day.

A storeroom off his kitchen is crowded with big covered vessels, most of them made of granite, which belong to his "regular customers" who call at his home to pick up tamales.

There is a rack at the bottom of the vessels on which the tamales are placed vertically to steam. Boiling water is under the rack.

"Most of my regular customers got two vessels," said Early. "If I know when they going to call, I can have the tamales hot and ready the next time."

Early's tamales come in six "pepper calibers," styled *A*, *B*, *C*, and *X*, *Y*, *Z*. *A* signifies a mildly pungent one, and *Z* stands for one "hot enough to burn through a hinge."

The Tamale King is often pressed for his recipe. He always answers: "Wouldn't do you no good if I gave you it. You wouldn't have the time and patience to pick nothing but Number One corn shucks and then cull them. This isn't very good corn country, and sometimes Number One shucks is scarce as pure religion. You wouldn't have time to spend six hours over a wood stove. For making a Western Union tamale is like driving on the highway. If you go too slow or too fast you is breaking the law.

"I learned to make tamales from my brother-in-law, Lincoln Vaughn, an old-timey railroad cook. This was around 1916 and I was young and didn't get so sincerely about it at first. They is two classes of hound dogs, a ketch dog and a hold dog. A ketch dog is good but a hold dog is better. I was just a ketch dog between 1916 and 1919. Then, after getting out of the First World's War I got more sincerely. As far as tamales was figured in it, I become a hold dog.

"So, ever since I got sincerely, I been selling tamales on Tuesdays, Thursdays, and Saturdays, on my corner in front of the Reliance Gas Company building."

Since 1919, Early has owned only two automobiles, a 1917 Model T Ford, and a Model A Ford which he bought secondhand in 1932 and which still serves him well.

One of his rich boyhood friends, Clint Murchison, Sr., offered to buy him a new car and take it out in tamales. Early declined.

"Was I to get me a new car, I might get trifling. I might get less sincerely, and The King can't be that way. The Model A is the greatest car in the world for my business. I don't use it for nothing but to fetch my tamales to my corner and to prowl around in the country, looking for blackjack oak for my stove and for Number One corn shucks.

"Nobody want to ride with me, because they know they get

all the meanness shook out of them. They ain't but two people on earth who can make a real tamale, and I'm both of them. But to keep being The King I needs my Model A car and my wood stove."

Early has a sense of dynasty. He worries about who will be his successor as "The World's Greatest Tamale King." He said his medical doctor "been doctoring for arthritis, but other day he tell me, 'Early, you ain't really got to worry about your arthritis — you got to worry about your old-age-itis'."

He gave early training in tamale making to a young relative and had considered the lad the heir to his business. Only the youth got into a scrape and wound up in the state penitentiary. The nephew was pardoned later by a Texas governor and is now assisting Early as "The Crown Prince of Hot Tamale Makers."

Early has many influential friends. He said he had a prominent tamale customer of his "writing to Governor Connally to see if something can be did about getting that boy out of the pen.

"Time is getting short. The King got to teach that boy all there is to know about making a Western Union hot tamale."

Most towns in the Southwest have, or had, "tamale kings," although few are as dedicated as Early Caldwell. Usually, they were of Mexican or Negro ancestry. The best tamale makers in the Texas hill country are of German or Czech ancestry, although they don't often peddle them from a handcart, wagon, or car.

John Floore of Helotes, Texas, in the hills above San Antonio, was the only fellow I knew who peddled tamales in a new Cadillac. For years John's tamales were made by Cora Sitter of Rio Medina, and Mr. Floore rates this lady of German descent the best tamale maker of his experience.

Some of the most memorable ones, though, were blacks. As DeWitt Landis of Dallas, formerly of Lubbock, once wrote me: "Remember John Fair, the elderly black gentleman who used to sell tamales from a cart in Lubbock? Was anything ever better than old John's tamales?"

In recent times, Nacogdoches, in the East Texas pine forests, had a Negro tamale vendor who also sold corn whiskey of his own distilling, the jugs wrapped in newspaper, same as the tamales. His sales cry was: "Hot tamales! Hot tamales! And that ain't all!"

"He's one of the best tamale makers I've ever eaten after," said Bob Murphey, then the district attorney in Nacogdoches. "We sure couldn't stand to lose him. We didn't want to see him wasting his talents down in the state penitentiary. So I let him off with a warning that he'd better stop bootlegging, or else."

After that, the Nacogdoches artist turned his skills strictly to tamales and his new sales cry was: "Hot tamales! Hot tamales! and that's ALL!"

Unlike chili con carne, hot tamales definitely originated in Mexico and are still much appreciated there. *"Tamalli"* is an Aztec word. And the Indians were enjoying them when Hernando Cortés and his conquistadors burst rudely on the scene in 1519.

Main difference in hot tamales made in this country and in Mexico is that our tamales are usually much larger and tied with corn husks at both ends, while the smaller Mexican tamales are tied at only one end. Also, in this country only piquant meat fillings are used. In Mexico there is a vast variety of fillings, even sweet ones.

There are endless recipes for making Texas-style hot tamales. One of my relatives, Marcus Gist of Odessa, earned his way through Texas A&M making and selling hot tamales. Mark is a well-to-do rancher now, but he is still rated one of the best tamale makers in West Texas. He makes no secret about his recipe, saying: "The best one I've ever found is on the Gebhardt's chili powder can."

It takes time and hard work to make tamales in the ancient Indian way.

Shelled corn in boiled in quicklime — say three pounds of corn to three ounces of lime, with enough water to cover. Boil it until the outer cuticle of the grains of corn begins to peel. Put it in cool, fresh water so you can rub it with your hands until the outer skin comes off. Rinse until the corn is white. It is then hominy or *maíz molido*.

The original corn-grinding instruments were a *metate*, or small stone table, on the top of which the corn was placed, and a *mano*, or stone roller. The mano was rolled over the grains on the metate until you had meal. Or, if you still insist on doing it this way, you can grind it out fine in a food chopper.

Instant masa is the best thing that has happened to the women of Mexico. A United States firm helped Mexican engineers develop a process for making instant masa. The firm, Quaker Oats, was rewarded by being given a license to make and sell instant masa in the United States. You can find Masa Harina in most big food stores.

To make the tamale paste, the three pounds of ground corn are mixed with a pound of shortening and worked into a creamy state. You use just enough water to make it come out in the consistency of a thick paste. For better-flavored paste, use the broth saved from making the tamale's meat filling.

The suggested ingredients for the meat filling are: 6 pounds of lean beef (although half pork and half beef can be the vehicle); ½ cup of rendered beef suet; 1 large onion; 4 garlic cloves chopped; 1 tablespoon of salt; 1 teaspoon of orégano; and ¾ cup of chili powder or, better still, 4 to 8 red chili pods in the pulp stage, same as when making the pulp for chili con carne.

Boil the meat until tender. Of course, you'll need a rather large pot. As suggested, pour the broth off and save it for use in the masa paste and in the meat filling. Cut the meat into bite-size pieces or smaller. Combine the meat, enough of the broth to turn the whole thing into a very thick meat gravy, and the rendered suet, the onion, garlic, and spices, and the chili powder or chili pepper pulp. Bring it all to a boil, stirring to keep it from sticking. Cook it until the tender meat has become done. Probably 10 minutes of boiling should accomplish this.

By Number One corn shuck, Early Caldwell says he means a stout one about six inches long and three inches wide, and he comments: "You can make a short shuck out of a long shuck, but you sure can't make a long shuck out of a short one."

Boil about two pounds of corn shucks for an hour. Remove the silk and rinse well in warm water. Stand each shuck upright to drain and dry.

Early reserves about half of the shuck on the left-hand side for spreading the masa paste, although he leaves enough at the top and the bottom not pasted so he can tie the ends with corn husks. He spreads on the paste about an eighth of an inch thick. He cools the meat filling before spreading it on top of the masa, so it won't run. How much meat filling you put in depends on your own preference and the capacity of the shuck.

Early says he rolls the shuck then, with its paste and meat filling, "just like I roll a cigarette." Some tamale makers spread a thin icing of paste on a second and smaller shuck and use it as a binder around the midriff of the tamale. If he suspects that a shuck isn't strong enough to hold his generous fillings, Early wraps several shucks around the tamale, each one covering the seam of the shuck underneath, before he ties up the bundle.

"Was a shuck to bust you really got a mess in the steamer," said Early.

As already noted, the covered vessels, preferably of granite, but aluminum will serve, have racks in the bottom on which the tamales are stacked vertically, not touching, to steam. The rack must be above the boiling water you pour in the bottom. The tamales steam for at least an hour.

The shucks are very, very important in flavoring the tamale. "Without *hojas de maíz,* the tamale she is nothing." says Tony Hernandez of the Alamo Grocery Store in Dallas. For a while, some makers of canned tamales were, outrageously, wrapping them in paper, but this sin seems to be on the decline among the canners.

As for enchiladas, you could write a long essay on the various ways they are prepared in Mexico. Some of the best enchiladas I've ever had were in a little café in Múzquiz, Mexico, and the ingredients included back country-style cottage cheese, or clabber cheese as it was called in my childhood, and a very hot red chili pepper sauce.

This book will be concerned, however, only with Southwest-style enchiladas, the kind usually prepared by "Anglo" cooks.

The best enchiladas I know about in this category were served at Joe Banks' Café, in Dallas, now, sad to say, closed because the land was needed for a park.

Mrs. Banks is a relative of the Schliepake family, owners of the oldest continuously operated restaurant in the Southwest, The Blue Front, also in Dallas. Besides German food, The Blue Front has been a temple of superlative chili.

There once was a "chili rivalry" between these kinsmen. Both the Schliepakes and the Bankses claimed to serve the best chili in town. You couldn't go wrong at either place.

Melvin Belli, the San Francisco lawyer, became extremely fond of Mrs. Banks' chili and enchiladas. While he was in Dallas to defend Jack Ruby at the famous trial, Belli had lunch several times a week at the Banks' place, and almost always he had either or both of the two fiery entrees. He became as "hooked" on Mrs. Banks' chili as Liz Taylor is on Dave Chasen's chili. After the trial, Belli had Mrs. Banks airfreight frozen chili to him in San Francisco. And a bowl of red would often inspire a glowing telegram to Mrs. Banks.

Not many things in Dallas during the trial pleased Belli — but the Banks' chili sure did.

Mrs. Banks' enchiladas are very simple to make — if you

have her wonderful version of chili con carne and fresh, soft tortillas as a starter. She softens the tortillas in hot grease — for just a few seconds. The tortillas are then put on a dry cloth, paper towel, or waxed paper. Put two teaspoons of chopped onions and two teaspoons of grated cheese on each tortilla, and roll. (Note: Mrs. Banks uses yellow "rat cheese," never "wheel cheese" or the so-called longhorn cheese which has a tendency to be stringy.)

The tortilla rolls are placed on a platter and covered with thick, meaty chili. Never use chili with beans. Sprinkle grated cheese heavily over the chili con carne. Place in a very hot oven and heat until cheese is melted and lightly browned.

Probably the best Mexican-style food along the Tex-Mex border is found at the Old Borunda. This is a restaurant in Marfa, Texas, which, as the cliché goes, has been an "institution" for more than sixty-five years.

In the kitchen and doing all the cooking is a remarkable woman, Mrs. Caroline Borunda Humphries, the owner since 1938. Before that, for many decades, the café was operated by Mrs. Humphries' mother, Mrs. Rosa Borunda.

It's in a white, stuccoed abode building in downtown Marfa. There's a narrow, well-kept garden between the building and the street with trees crowding against the adobe walls, one a tall pine and the other a high, fleecy tree described as a wild weeping willow. The interior of Old Borunda is always a dazzling, freshly painted white. The plain chairs and tables also seem always freshly painted. The décor would be almost like that in a science laboratory if it weren't for the many oil paintings on the walls, two of them being studies of Mrs. Humphries' ranch home; and if it weren't for the haunting, peppery smells from the kitchen.

Mrs. Humphries operates only "every other day" and on short hours schedules "because to keep the food always good I have to be always in the kitchen. I might hire a cook as dedicated as I. But then he might quit."

She usually opens around 5 P.M. and closes "when I run

out of food." In 1955 when Elizabeth Taylor was in a movie
called *Giant,* she lived for several weeks in Marfa. (The film
was being shot mostly on a nearby ranch.) Miss Taylor
became a regular patron at Old Borunda. Elizabeth Taylor
expressed her appreciation of the fare with an autographed
picture, but Caroline never hung it on her café's walls.

The most expensive full course dinner at Old Borunda was
still $2.50 in 1982.

Enrique Vásquez, who operates an excellent Mexican food
restaurant in Uvalde, Texas, is a long-time judge and scorekeeper at the chili contests in Terlingua. Twenty is a perfect
score in the chili wars, and few question Enrique's math-
ematics when he's performing as scorekeeper, since he does
all his figuring in Spanish.

In his own kitchen Enrique makes delicious armadillo meat
chili and also uses armadillo meat as a base for tamales. Of
course, he's not permitted to use armadillo meat in his café.
But he makes up hundreds of armadillo meat salad finger
sandwiches for church dances and other social events. Most
of the people at the dances eat the finger sandwiches with
relish, thinking they are made of chicken or pork. Enrique
hangs armadillo meat in his restaurant cooler for two weeks
of aging, same as he does beef. And he thinks this is a big help
in improving the flavor of wild game such as armadillos,
although these little armored creatures have such passive
personalities perhaps "wild" is the wrong word.

Not much scholarly research has been done on the Mexican sandwich called *burrito.* No one seems to know why it was
so named since *burrito* means a small donkey or a burro
junior grade.

The burrito in the culinary sense is a cousin of the taco.
The main difference is that the burrito has a wheat flour
tortilla for a packaging while the taco has a corn meal or
Masa Harina tortilla for a casing. Also, in the burrito the
tortilla is often folded quite tightly. The taco cartridge is

more like a shell. The burrito crust is more pie-like.

Celso, the No. 1 waiter in the elegant Arturo's Restaurant in Nuevo Progreso, Mexico, on the Rio Grande near Mc-Allen, Texas, told me that he believes the burrito was developed in Mexico's state of Sonora. "In Sonora they no like corn so much for making the tortilla. They love flour torillas. And to make the burritos they put in all kinds of fillings, frijoles, beef, guacamole, chicken, fish, or even marinated cracklings."

14. "The Gentleman from Odessa," or Son-of-a-Bitch Stew

"If a son-of-a-bitch stew don't have marguts it ain't a son-of-a-bitch."

Old range cook saying

A student at the University of Texas, Miss Catherine Young, once wrote an essay in praise of son-of-a-bitch stew. This was in a course taught by J. Frank Dobie. Professor Dobie gave her an A-plus on the paper.

Miss Young, now Mrs. Edward E. Clack of Burkburnett, Texas, began the essay with a reference to the 1836 Texas revolutionists under General Sam Houston, who, at the Battle of San Jacinto, "seized this land [Texas] from the powers that were [the Mexican government], called it their own, and justified their unpardonable conduct to themselves and to posterity in the name of righteousness."

After this controversial comment on the Texas Revolution, she continued: "Decade by decade I have followed the Texans' career. I have searched for a peculiar contribution which they might have made to civilization . . . They robbed and prayed and fought and died; it is no new chronicle. What have we that the Spartans lacked, that the Roman Centurion knew not, that the Puritan needed and the Yankee ignores?"

She then declared that Texas' greatest contribution to civilization was son-of-a-bitch stew:

"Made of unmentionables, it is the *pièce de résistance* of the chuck wagon. What matter the ingredients when the result is a culinary poem . . . It is the Sacrament of the Plains, the recompense of hardy men and daring women. It is the grand contribution of the prairies to the Valhalla of Gourmets!"

A legend has it that S.O.B. acquired its vigorous title long ago when an Eastern visitor at a Texas ranch asked one of the cowboys: "What was in that delicious stew the cook just served me?"

"I'll be a son-of-a-bitch if I know all that goes into it. Different cooks put in different things, but it's sure good," replied the cowboy. "One thing in there for sure is margut."

Marrow gut, called "margut" by the old cooks, is the decisive ingredient, the one which gives S.O.B. its unforgettable flavor.

There was a saying: "A son-of-a-bitch might have no brains and no heart and still be a son-of-a-bitch. But if it don't have no guts, it's not a son-of-a-bitch."

Actually, the marrow gut is neither marrow nor gut. It is the long tube connecting the two stomachs of cud-chewing creatures. It is edible only if the calf hasn't been weaned. At least the "marrow" part of the phrase is explained by the fact that the tube is very tender and tastes like marrow — before the calf starts eating grass.

Marrow gut, called *tripa de leche* by Spanish-speaking folk, is considered quite a delicacy when cooked alone. In the cattle country it is sometimes roasted on a stick or cut into rings, rolled in flour, and fried.

A range cook would require an average-size, unweaned

calf for the ingredients to make the stew for ten to a dozen cowhands. These things would go into the concoction: all of the marrow gut, or at least a 3-foot length of it; all of the calf's brains; all of the sweetbreads; ½ of the heart; all of the butcher steak — lean strips of meat inside the ribs; ⅓ of the liver (go slow on the liver or leave it out); ½ of the melt, a ductless gland back of the floating kidney; 2 or 3 cups of rendered beef kidney suet; the oxtail soup bone; the calf's tongue (this is also optional and a lot of trouble, for you have to skin it and it's tough to cube); 2 pounds of brisket or stew meat.

All the meat except the brains is cut into sizes about the same as if you were making chili, although Chalma Reid of the Pitchfork Ranch, one of the senior wagon cooks of the West, cubes the meat even finer.

The liver can spoil the stew if it is too bitter. If you decide to use it sparingly, boil the liver 30 or 40 minutes by itself before adding it to the stew.

Also, boil the oxtail soup bone until the meat comes from the bones. Add the meat from the soup bone to the stew meat.

Chalma Reid seasons the meat lightly with salt and sage and heavily with black pepper and crushed red pepper. Seasoning is a matter of personal preference. On the King Ranch, and other spreads in Southwest Texas, the cooks often throw in a lot of chilipiquines or other hot peppers.

Some cooks put the cubes of heart and tongue in a pot and boil them first, as these are the toughest ingredients. Some wait until the last half hour of cooking the whole mixture to add the brains, which dissolve quickly. Chalma Reid has the brains in the pot all the way, to add thickening.

Just enough water is put over the meat to cover. It is then cooked slowly for 3 and 4 hours, or until throroughly done and tender.

Chalma Reid (there will be more on his long career with the chuck wagons in this book), says: "S.O.B. shouldn't boil much. Just simmer. Hardest thing for the womenfolk in making S.O.B. is the standing around to see that it simmers and don't boil."

The wagon cooks through the years have never weakened S.O.B.'s protein power by dropping in vegetables, such as tomatoes, onions, and potatoes. As composed by artists such as Chalma Reid of the Pitchfork, this is an all-beef symphony — a composition of the cheapest and most vitamin-packed cuts.

Mr. Reid cooked on the range for more than a half century. He seldom made a stew for less than ten cowboys.

At my request, though, Chalma took pen in hand and tried to figure out the weights and measures for S.O.B. for four or five persons: ½ pound of boneless chuck or rounds of beef; ½ pound of rendered beef suet; 1½ pounds of marrow gut; ¾ pound of beef heart; ⅓ pound of liver (optional); ¾ pound of calf sweetbreads; one set of calf brains with the membrane removed. This is cooked in the same way as the previously described stew for a dozen cowboys.

Blondie Young, a tall, reddish-haired fellow in his sixties, who looks much younger, was for many years range cook for the Four Sixes Ranch, which adjoins the Pitchfork. One time I was at the Four Sixes fall roundup and Blondie had some leisure to reminisce: "They's cooks, such as old Chalma Reid over on the Pitchfork, who has cooked son-of-a-bitches longer than I have. But I bet no one ever cooked a bigger son-of-a-bitch.

"I worked for the Waggoner Ranch for thirty-eight years. Old Dan Waggoner, the founder of the Three D, was the fondest fellow of S.O.B. I have ever knowed. It was his fav-o-right. One time he invited more than three hundred folks to eat. I used a herd of unweaned calves to make the stew. And Mr. Dan said it was not only the biggest S.O.B. he ever saw cooked, but one of the best."

Who made the first S.O.B. stew? Probably the Plains Indians, those who lived where vegetation was sparse. Take the case of the Comanche Indians of the Staked Plain in the Texas Panhandle and eastern New Mexico: in the winter months they lived mostly on meat. They didn't know anything about vitamins, but they knew that steaks and roasts and ribs, the conventional cuts of meat, lacked something. They found this something in the vital organs of buffalo, deer, antelope, and elk — the hearts, livers, melts, brains, testicles (the last is still used in some S.O.B. recipes).

On the cattle drives from Texas to Kansas, the trail cooks had many contacts with Plains Indians, whom they saw eating with relish the parts of beef which many people threw away. The chuck wagons on the trail seldom carried any kind of vegetables, and, like the Comanches in the winter months, the cowhands would develop a craving that was only satisfied by eating what came to be the ingredients for S.O.B. stew.

My granduncle, John M. (Uncle Johnny) Gist, had ranches, at various times, in the Panhandle, near Marfa in the Big Bend, and near Odessa near the bend of the New Mexico border. Usually, he was based at Odessa, at least in the last four decades of his life.

This old trail driver was also twice president of the American Hereford Breeders. At one fat stock show he was introduced as "The Gentleman from Odessa." I asked him about this.

"Oh, that announcer was just calling me a son-of-a-bitch in a nice way," replied the old cowman. "When Odessa first became a town, it was considered a pretty rough town — with lots of mean men running around loose. Some of the neighboring towns considered the early Odessa pretty uncivilized. These towns had a joke. They said a gentleman in Odessa would be a son-of-a-bitch anyplace else."

In the olden days, menus of cafés in West Texas and eastern New Mexico sometimes had an entree printed as "Gentleman from Odessa Stew." This was a polite way of listing S.O.B.

Sometimes, the menus listed S.O.B. under the name of a personage currently in public disfavor. For example, after President Grover Cleveland ran the cattlemen out of the Cherokee Strip, some cafés started printing it "Grover Cleveland Stew." In the depression of the 1930s it was styled "Herbert Hoover Stew."

In the years just before World War I, a Texas governor and his lady went to a dinner dance in Van Horn in the Diablo Mountains, west of El Paso. Son-of-a-bitch stew was the only meat course. The governor's lady, after she learned what went into this particular stew (included were the marrow gut and testicles of bighorn sheep from the Diablos), declined to eat it.

There were few women for the dancing after dinner. The governor's lady was much in demand as a partner. Near dawn the poor woman was having her feet stepped on by a booted and spurred, tobacco-chewing rancher, who asked her: "How did you like the S.O.B.?"

"I didn't eat any," she replied. "I've danced with a few, though, tonight."

15. The Pitchfork's Cook and Some "Hoods"

"You can have that cooking in the rain and snow. I liked a canvas wall to break the wind."

Chalma Reid,
former Pitchfork Ranch range cook

"Me and my hood make a home on the range for twenty-one cowboys, seven or eight months out of each year," said Chalma Reid, wagon cook for the Pitchfork Ranch in northwestern Texas.

By "my hood," Mr. Reid meant his assistant, Henry Muriel, whose many duties include driving the hoodlum wagon, auxiliary vehicle to the chuck wagon.

The Pitchfork's three-pronged brand goes back to 1881, and the ranch is now 267,000 acres on the headwaters of the Brazos River in a raw red country of canyons and mesas interspersed with broad, grassy vegas.

On the ranch there is usually a basic herd of four thousand mother cows and all the bulls that are needed. And, added to the immense calf crops, thousands of steers are often in residence.

Chalma Reid was still healthy and agile when he retired in his late seventies, and at the time was the dean of his profession. Mr. Reid is a tall, white-haired man with courtly manners. He couldn't be treated with more respect by the cowboys if he were the proprietor of the ranch or majority leader of the United States Senate.

The Pitchfork has a smaller ranch in Wyoming. Some of the veteran Pitchfork cowboys have worked all over the West. All of them maintain that "Mister Reid," as they always addressed him, was the most talented, versatile cook of their range experience.

As on most ranches operated in the old-fashioned way, about sixty feet in all directions around the chuck wagon is "cook's territory." You must not ride a horse into cook's territory, for you might fetch along a cloud of dust to settle on food in preparation. And should any cowboy be so rude and ignorant as to tie his horse to the chuck wagon, Chalma would lose his temper. He might even react as did an old *cocinero* on a neighboring ranch years ago. A rookie cowhand tied his pony to the chuck wagon wheel. The irate cook simply jerked the bridle off the animal and set the pony to galloping off with a slap on the rump.

Today on most of the big flatland cattle spreads, the chuck wagons are motorized trucks. The Pitchfork and its neighboring ranch, the Four Sixes (the brand celebrates a winning poker hand), are among the few outfits who still use the old-fashioned, mule-drawn chuck wagons.

"The wagon is out" is a phrase on the Pitchfork which means that a roundup is in progress. This goes on for about four months in the fall and winter and for a similar time span starting in late February or early March. And, when the wagon is out, wagon boss B. G. Drennan and his cowboys work from "can to can't," meaning they saddle up the first of a relay of horses in the earliest morning light and are still in the saddle at dusk or later.

This goes on for seven days a week during the roundups except, as the wagon boss phrases it, "for a few Sundays when we don't have cattle to hold and can take off for a spell."

There are usually about a half-dozen married cowboys who live in cottages at the ranch headquarters and are permitted to go home nights when the chuck wagon hasn't stopped in terrain too rugged to be reached by a four-wheel-drive truck. The single cowhands spend each night in their bedrolls.

So, for most of the Pitchfork cowboys, the chuck wagon is home for seven to eight months out of the year.

On the roundups, Chalma Reid drove the chuck wagon. This is an ordinary ranch wagon to which have been attached several boxes containing drawers and compartments for carrying supplies. The biggest of these boxes is the chuck box, bolted onto the rear of the wagon. It has a hinged cover or lid which opens down from the top to form a large table, after stout "legs" are dropped into support.

This lid-table may also be supported by ropes or chains from the top. The work table is for the exclusive use of the cook, and not even the wagon boss dares to lay a cup of coffee on it.

Some say that Colonel Charles Goodnight, the first major cattleman in the Texas Panhandle, invented the chuck wagon while he was blazing the Goodnight-Loving trail into New Mexico. Anyway, the chuck wagon was invented in the years just after the War Between the States when the great cattle drives started from Texas to the northern railroads and markets.

The old emigrant wagons were too ponderous, and, if pulled by oxen, were slower than the cow herds. A horse-or mule-drawn vehicle was needed which was stout enough to carry supplies to sustain dozens of cowboys through hundreds of miles of wilderness and still compact and fast enough that the cook-driver could get out ahead of the herd and have a hot meal ready when the crew came to a noon holding point or stopped for the night.

This wagon may have been named by Indians on the trail to Kansas who called it a "chuckaway wagon" and styled the cook the "chuckaway chief."

A trail cook had to be skilled and patient and imaginative. For he worked without shelter in all kinds of weather and with meager supplies. He might have only materials for making coffee, biscuits, frijoles (from dried beans, usually pintos), salt pork, and fresh beef. Often he also had bacon, dried fruit, molasses.

Canned goods in very limited variety appeared in the late nineteenth century. Cowpunchers became the first real aficionados of canned tomatoes. In country that was very dry or had bad water they often carried canned tomatoes as a substitute for water.

Canned condensed milk was much appreciated when the range cooks finally got it. There is an old jingle in praise of canned milk:

> No teats to pull, no hay to pitch;
> You just punch a hole in the son-of-a-bitch . . .

Chalma Reid came along after trail days. The range cooks were just as respected and appreciated as the old trail *cocineros*, though. Outfits were judged by the quality of their chuck wagon cookery. The competition was particularly keen when several big ranches pooled crews for cooperative roundups, and there was a confrontation of cooks. "Them boys would sure try to outdo each other then," said Chalma Reid.

Unlike Cap Warren of the Waggoner Ranch, Mister Reid isn't the least nostalgic for the days when he cooked in the open.

The Pitchfork has an "evangelist-style" tent, similar to the one which offended Cap Warren so much.

"You can have that cooking in the rain and snow. I liked a canvas wall to break the wind," said Chalma.

Henry Muriel, the hood, was the first out of his bedroll

each morning. By 4:30 A.M. he would have a roaring mesquite log fire reduced to huge glowing coals in the stove.

The first use Chalma had for the red coals was to make a huge pot of coffee, using at least one handful of ground coffee for each cup of water.

"Chalma's coffee sat up and walked and talked," said wagon boss Drennan. "It really woke you up."

The coals gave an even temperature for baking the marvelous sourdough biscuits and other hot breads for which Chalma Reid was famous.

There was hot bread at every meal. "I once knew a range cook who was called Cold Bread Bill," said Chalma, who first started cooking at the old "24" Ranch in Kent County, Texas. "Cold Bread Bill would save his leftover biscuits from breakfast and warm them over for dinner and supper. I don't aim to ever be called Cold Bread Chalma."

The 5 A.M.-or-earlier breakfast always included biscuits, coffee, syrup (but no butter), fried eggs — Chalma usually cooked sixty or more eggs for the wagon boss, the twenty-one cowboys, the cook, and the hood — and, most often, thickly sliced bacon.

On the Pitchfork's 267,000 acres there is a lot of wild game, including quail, dove, turkey, deer, and a few pronghorn antelopes. In season, Chalma often surprised his "boarders" with wild game entrees, such as fried or roasted quail in place of bacon.

In the canyons and red water courses there are wild plum thickets and vines of even wilder-tasting grapes, and Chalma made the fruits into excellent tart jellies and preserves in the summer before he went out on the range.

Most chuck wagon cooks never offer any sweetening except syrup and stewed, dried fruits. Chalma, however, in addition to the plum and grape jellies and preserves, also baked pies on the portable stove, his specialties being mince pies, made from venison or pronghorn meat, and pumpkin pies.

A Pitchfork cowboy would have been working for at least six hours and exhausted at least one horse by "dinner-time" at high noon. Around Chalma's chuck wagon, dinner was a more descriptive term for the noon meal than luncheon. In his endeavor to please the tastes of all the crew, the cook usually had two entrees for both the midday and the evening meals, the latter being called "supper."

At one of these meals, Mister Reid may have had both a huge beef roast, not cooked with vegetables, which he called "dry roast," and a savory stew with beef ribs the main ingredient.

After six hours in the saddle a cowboy likes a hearty side dish such as one which Chalma labels "drunkard's casserole." This is made in a small dishpan instead of a casserole and consists of alternate layers of Irish potatoes, sliced medium thick, and layers of thinly sliced Bermuda onions, with a thick stratum of sharp cheese on the top. This is baked long enough for the potatoes to become done but not so long that the onions become mushy.

Unique on the Pitchfork is a grilled version of son-of-a-bitch stew. To prepare this, Chalma would turn from his iron stove to a pit dug in the ground near the chuck wagon by Henry the Hood. The hood fired up a big bed of mesquite chunk coals in the pit, and laid enough branding irons over the sides to support a flat piece of steel, which was the grill.

The same ingredients were used for the grilled version, only the meat was finely sliced rather than cut into chili-bite-size chunks. It was all scrambled and cooked like eggs.

"Takes only thirty minutes or a little over for a grilled son-of-a-bitch where you stand for hours over a stew, and the boys can't seem to get enough of it," said Mister Reid.

The Pitchfork cowboys continue to gather cattle right up until a day or two before Christmas.

"The best eating of all the year from Chalma's wagon was between Thanksgiving Day and Christmas," said wagon boss Drennan. "Then Mister Reid really tried to outdo hisself.

You haven't really eaten turkey until you had tried the roasted wild ones Mister Reid pulled from that portable stove, and no one, we say, could bake a better mince or pumpkin pie."

During the roundups, Chalma often broiled or fried thick steaks, from ranch coolers, on the iron stove. During the gastronomical festival between Thanksgiving Day and Christmas, he took the time to broil steaks across branding irons over sweet-smelling mesquite logs in a pit.

Like Cap Warren, Chalma started out as a cowboy, but had been taught to cook well by his mother. He took the chuck wagon job as a temporary thing — he thought.

"I was doing well as a cowboy on the old "24" Ranch in 1910 when the *cocinero* th'owed a big drunk and got fired. I thought I was taking the cooking job just a few days, but they liked my cooking, and I've never gone back to cowboying."

Mister Reid had never "lived in town" until he was about seventy years old.

"I got to studying about how it would be to live in town and sleep late until about five-thirty or six o'clock, and in a real bed, not no bedroll. I was fixed then so I didn't have to work no more, and I still am. So I told Mr. Dee Burns, then the Pitchfork manager, that I was retiring and moving to the city."

Mr. Burns, with much sadness, consented to the cook's retirement. Mister Reid said good-by to his hood and the cowboys. He drove off in his pickup truck and settled down in nearby Snyder, an oil and cattle town with a population of about 15,000.

Chalma was soon discontented. He explained it this way:

"Snyder is a mighty fine place if you like the bright lights and city life. Me, I guess I'm spoiled for ever making a town man. I get nervous and fidgety. Here I was a big, strong, willing man loafing around on town streets. I got to feeling so twilighty that, finally, I called Mr. Burns on the telephone and asked if I could come back. I told him I just plain missed the Pitchfork and my wagon."

"We've missed you even more, Chalma. Come on back,"
said Mr. Burns.

And a few days later, the white-haired, courtly old cook
was back presiding over the Pitchfork chuck wagon.

Chalma finally retired for good in 1968, and the Pitchfork
has had many range cooks since then.

Marcus Gist, once a range cook but now an Odessa millionaire, said that cowboys always couched their adverse
criticism of the cooking in diplomatic language for fear they
might be commissioned the *cocinero* if their gripes caused the
cook to be fired.

The complainers might phrase it this way: "The
sourdoughs is full of sand. The frijoles is so hard they rattle
in my plate. The coffee is weak and there's too much salt in
the son-of-a-bitch. But that's just how I like it."

Fuel was hard to come by on the plains. Marcus Gist said:
"When moving a herd, every cowpuncher who found a
mesquite root or any other kind of fuel would throw it on the
chuck wagon or the hood's cart. Because I was raised mostly
on the plains, I cooked more with cow chips than anything
else in the early days.

"If you have kerosene to start the chips to burning, and
plenty of wind, this dried cow manure makes a good hot fire.
You have to watch it, though. There has been more bread
burned in Dutch ovens heated by cow chips than by any kind
of wood."

This 'prairie coal" had one immense disadvantage. It
wouldn't burn in damp weather.

Evetts Haley, in his book on the immense XIT ("Ten
Counties in Texas") Ranch of the Panhandle and South
Plains of Texas, wrote that in the late nineteenth century in
that country, cow chips came to be called "Babcock coal," in
honor of a fastidious XIT executive.

"Colonel Babcock," wrote Haley, quoting a cowpuncher,

"had a very strong dislike for anything cooked with cow chips. His dislike for this fuel furnished the camp with a good deal of amusement and the boys soon began to refer to it as Babcock coal."

When I grew up on a ranch in the Texas Panhandle, we had a number of British neighbors. By this time, these people had become pretty acclimated to the country, and the new generation often spoke with pure Texas accents as contrasted with the clipped intonations of their elders. But when the Britishers, especially the many titled ones, first came to the Panhandle, they had a hard time getting used to the ranch custom of the proprietors and the help eating together.

Once in the early 1880s on the JA Ranch, the British owners, the Honorable John Adair and his lady, were much affronted when one of the cowhands, Cape Willingham, later a famous sheriff, came in and plopped down beside them at the big table and started eating with his knife serving the purposes of both fork and spoon.

"Really, old chap, we're not accustomed to eating with the servants," Adair told Cape.

The cowboy made an angry reply before he stalked out: "Here I am a boy who can ride anything that grows hair, and yet you say I ain't good enough to eat with you folks."

John Adair then accompanied the cowboys on roundups, only he slept on a cot in a comfortable tent. On a night of savage wind and rain, soon after the incident at the dinner table, Cape Willingham got his revenge. He galloped by the Adair tent, roped the top of it, and dragged the shelter off into the night, leaving the British gentleman exposed to the storm.

The Adairs soon learned Panhandle ways and became very democratic and popular.

Henry Muriel, the Pitchfork hood, was a stocky, poker-faced, middle-aged fellow.

Besides driving the hoodlum wagon, the auxiliary vehicle

to the chuck wagon, Henry the Hood had many duties, such as making the cook and branding-iron fires, putting up and taking down the tent, chopping mesquite firewood, washing dishes. The hoodlum wagon carries posthole diggers, branding irons, carpenter tools, axes, the tent, and all of the bedrolls that can't be put on the chuck wagon. Henry was also in charge of keeping the camp supplied with water.

The Book of Joshua described range hoods: "Let them be hewers of wood and drawers of water unto all the congregation . . ."

The range hoods never presume to dress in the boots, leather chaps, and big sombreros of the working cowboys. Instead, they look like farm laborers in their flat shoes and khaki work clothes.

Bob Murphey of Nacogdoches, Texas, once remarked that "a hood, among all those fancy-dressed cowboys, must feel like a one-eyed mule at a quarter-horse show."

One of the most colorful of the hoods was Zack Reid, who was senior employee of the Waggoner Ranch when he retired around 1959.

Long after the rest of the roundup crews had been pretty much mechanized, Zack continued to drive his hoodlum wagon, which was pulled by two ornery mules. Zack was a small fellow who somehow always seemed to have a three-day growth of reddish whiskers. He spoke seldom and then rather indistinctly except for the profanity. One of his claims: "I've built more cook fires and branding-iron fires than any man who ever lived."

For some reason, the mules that pulled Zack's wagon were always intractable. Once Zack loped his team up as close to the chuck wagon as the cook (Cap Warren) would let him. Zack jumped off the hoodlum wagon, throwing his reins to the ground, and went for a cup of coffee. Someone asked him if he wasn't afraid that his mules would run away. Zack replied: "Let the sons-o'-bitches run away. They got half a million acres to run in."

This just about summed up Zack the Hood's philosophy of life.

Henry Muriel hadn't been hood at the Pitchfork for long, although he had followed the vanishing profession most of his adult life. Chalma Reid's long-time hood, Slug Mayo, died in the early 1960s. Slug's cheerful philosophy is well remembered in the cow camps.

For example, he once said: "Before the Second World's War, I worked for a cowman who wouldn't hire a hand who both smoked Bull Durham cigarettes and wore a straw hat. He figured such a cowboy wouldn't get much work done, for when he wasn't rolling Bull he'd be chasing his hat."

After Chalma Reid retired, the Pitchfork had a tough time finding a replacement. Once they were so desperate that they hired the former chef at a famous New York City restaurant.

"He took a notion he wanted some fresh air," said Pitchfork manager Humphreys. The New York chef soon regretted his decision after he'd cooked for a few days on a wood stove from the hind end of a wagon drawn by four mules, although he wasn't required to drive the mules as old Chalma had done for so many years.

"We sure got tired of them soufflés which was his specialty," said wagon boss Drennan. "And he got tireder of us."

"He favored boiling beef instead of frying it or broiling it over coals," said one of the Pitchfork's senior cowboys, Buck Craft.

Manager Humphreys finally sent the New York chef to the Pitchfork's ranch in Wyoming "to cook for the hay hands. Before he quit up there he'd learned from Old Reno, the wagon cook in Wyoming, how to make pretty fair biscuits."

The most recent chuck wagon *cocinero* at the Pitchfork, and a really talented one, is Richard Bolt. When cigarette advertising was permitted on television, the Pitchfork and the adjoining ranch, the Four Sixes, were used as the scenes for filming elaborate commercials for Marlboro cigarettes. And Pitchfork and Four Sixes cowboys took roles in these films. In 1971 the cigarette company put out a booklet called "Chuck Wagon Cooking from Marlboro Country" in which the recipes of Richard Bolt were supposedly used. When last I saw Mr. Bolt the tall cook said:

"I'd sure appreciate if you would straighten out some of the recipes of mine they fouled up in that advertising book. The receipt for son-of-a-bitch stew especially needs correcting. I took pen in hand and wrote it down plain and then my wife typed it out that margut (marrow gut) is the most important taste ingredient in son-of-a-bitch stew. If you don't have margut you don't have a son-of-a-bitch. And yet that young home economics-type lady cook the advertising agency sent down from Chicago to take down my directions on wagon cooking just flat left out the margut and instead put something in I'd never drop in an S.O.B., a quarter pound of salt pork."

He studied the handsome thirteen-page booklet (with many ranch scenes, mostly of Bolt around the wagon) and continued: "That young lady from Chicago also left out the lights and melts in the stew. It's easy to get margut and lights and melts since most butchers throw them away, and I wouldn't think of putting carrots and onions in an S.O.B. either. She left out the chilies in my chili con carne recipe, and she was mighty mistaken in saying I add black coffee in my barbecue sauce."

16. Black-Eyed Peas and Pinto Beans

"There is no better way to start a day than to drink a large glass of cold black-eye pea pot likker, laced with pepper sauce."

The late Allen Duckworth

Outside of the Southwest and parts of the Old South, the black-eyed pea is the most "misunderstood" vegetable in this nation. To illustrate, Webster's International Dictionary insults the black-eyed pea by defining it as "the seed of a tropical vine used in the West Indies as food; also the cowpea."

This definition completely ignores the fact that tons of black-eyed peas, cooked in a perfect culinary union with salt pork, ham hock, or bacon sides, are consumed annually in more enlightened regions of the United States.

In the northeastern and midwestern states, black-eyed peas are raised for stock feed and are called cowpeas, same as in Webster's. When simply boiled in water, black-eyes *are* an uninteresting, although energy-packed dish. The secret is in the cooking. And we'll start off with a standard recipe:

132

The ingredients are: 3 cups of shelled, snapped fresh black-eyes; ¼ pound of salt pork, ham hock, or bacon ends; ½ teaspoon of salt; and water to cover.

The peas should be washed through several waters. Boil the peas with the rest of the ingredients for 15 minutes, then simmer until the peas are plump and tender. Try not to overcook them, though, for there is nothing worse than mushy black-eyes. Add only as much water as is needed. Keep the "pot likker" (liquor) as rich as possible.

My own favorite black-eye recipe calls for Virginia ham or bacon instead of the salt pork.

There are hundreds of ways to make them more delightful after they're cooked. Helen Corbitt, the Neiman-Marcus food consultant, is believed to be the innovator of "Texas Caviar," heavily spiced and pickled or preserved black-eyes. You can also make a "black-eyed pea dip" by mashing the peas and adding seasonings such as grated onion, garlic juice, Worcestershire, Tabasco, or pepper sauce, lemon juice, and either sour cream or mayonnaise.

Another Dallas authority, the late Allen Duckworth, ate nothing but black-eyes on certain days. Here Mr. Duckworth describes a typical menu:

"There is no better way to start a day than to drink a large glass of cold black-eye pea pot likker, laced with pepper sauce.

"A light noonday meal may consist of black-eyed pea cocktail, prepared in the same way as a shrimp cocktail, only with firm, tender peas instead of the shrimp. This is followed by black-eyed pea sandwiches: very soft homemade bread buttered generously, and spread with a thick layer of cold black-eyes, topped with thinly sliced Bermuda onion.

"The heavy meal at night is the time for rejoicing in the happy home where the black-eyed pea is supreme. Two dishes should be ready — pounds and pounds of black-eyes in a huge bowl, and a gallon of hot pot likker in a large pitcher. At each place there should be big plate for the peas, and a soup bowl for the pot likker. Break out an ovenful of hot corn bread, plenty of country butter, and cold buttermilk to wash it down. Then you're all set."

The man most responsible for removing the "hillbilly food" image from black-eyed peas and for spreading good recipes all over the civilized world was Elmore Torn of Taylor, Texas. He was an internationally recognized chemurgist who has gone all over the earth for the United States government to study food problems.

Elmore Torn, father of the actor Rip Torn, is the founder and president of the National Black-Eyed Pea Association. This should really be called the International Black-Eyed Pea Association, for it has members in four foreign countries. At last count, the membership was about ten thousand, with forty-seven states of the nation represented. As a measure of the missionary work done by Mr. Torn, the NBEPA has more members in states such as New York, Pennsylvania, California, and Oregon than in Texas, where, according to the NBEPA president, "people take the black-eyed pea for granted."

There are only two requirements for membership: (1) you must be a friend of the black-eyed pea, and (2) you must pay the postage for the recipes and proclamations which President Torn sends out annually.

Mr. Torn has invited food experts all over the country to join, and the only one ever to refuse was Bert Fireman of Phoenix, Arizona, a writer and cactus-jelly maker, who replied:

"Mr. Torn, I've never imbibed so much on New Year's Eve that I'd be so insensitive or indiscreet as to attempt to eat a mess of black-eyed peas decorated with chunks of sowbelly on the day following. Why start the year with such an alien taste? Why risk indigestion at a time when one's innards are already sorely tried by overindulgence?"

Mr. Fireman admitted that he'd never sampled black-eyed peas — "only looked at them."

Black-eyed pea producers from California to Virginia revere Elmore Torn because he is largely responsible for reviving an ancient superstition that it is lucky to eat black-eyed peas, or similar lentils, on New Year's Day.

This was an old Southern tradition. And during his travels as a chemurgist, Mr. Torn found that "the serving of some kind of black-eyed lentil is a New Year's Day custom in such places as Egypt, France, and India.

"One explanation," he said, "is that these lentils are great soil builders. Ask any farmer. You plant black-eyed peas for a few years and they restore soil worn out, for instance, by long cotton cultivation. So this business of the legume restoring the soil may have something to do with the superstition that black-eyes bring good luck for all the year."

Incidentally, Mr. Torn was haunted by the nickname of "King Nebuchadnezzar." This is because, about a quarter of a century ago, he took off fifty unneeded pounds by going on an all-grass (grass pills) diet for sixty-six days.

He reduced to a proper weight on this grass diet without ill effects to his health, and he didn't wind up in the physical condition of the Babylonian monarch, described in the fourth chapter of the Book of Daniel: "The same hour was the thing fulfilled upon Nebuchadnezzar: and he was driven from men, and did eat grass as oxen, and his body was wet with the dew of heaven, till his hairs were grown like eagles' feathers, and his nails like birds' claws."

Much was written on this diet in the newspapers, and Mr. Torn said he wouldn't try it again because of the "notoriety, even abroad. When I was over in Europe on my last food mission, I told a stranger I was from Taylor, Texas, and this fellow commented: 'Oh, that is the town where the chemurgist went off his rocker and lived on grass for two months. Do you know him'?"

One of chemurgist Elmore Torn's foreign missions was to go to Vietnam to see if the black-eyed pea would thrive there. The Texan was sponsored by some U.S. religious organizations who were attempting to improve and make more various the food crops of South Vietnam.

The war was then raging. The countryside was certainly unsafe. So Tiger Torn established his agricultural experimental project in a leper colony. Why? The answer is that the back country of South Vietnam was then controlled by the Vietcong and these guerrillas avoided leper colonies. During his worldwide work, Torn had picked up some languages, including a fair command of French. He developed a dreadful jungle fungus, which malady helped him in his role of a French priest with leprosy.

He was bold in his masquerade. Torn chewed tobacco. Once a Vietcong infantryman asked him: "What are you chewing on, leper?"

"Tobacco," said Torn, "and I spit in people's eyes with it."

He then had the audacity to spit in the face of the guerrilla. The latter told Torn: "If you weren't an old fool of a French leper I would use my rat-a-tat-tat [machine gun] on you."

Son Rip Torn sent supplies of smoked bacon, which somehow got through. And Elmore cooked big pots of peas, flavored by the smoked meat. The Vietnamese lepers became quite fond of black-eyed peas.

The lepers called Elmore Torn "Mr. Nuac Mam." *Nuac mam* is a powerful-smelling fish sauce made by the Vietnamese. Mr. Torn liked *nuac mam* so much he brought back a year's supply when he returned to Texas. "It's full of proteins and I would never have made it for all those long months in the jungle if it hand't been for *nuac mam*," he said. "I even pour it on my black-eyed peas."

Mr. Torn's Operation Black-eyed Pea in Vietnam was a failure. While the crops always flourished at the start, they were soon destroyed by jungle insects.

Also, the Vietcong were becoming suspicious of the white man who worked so vigorously in the fields.

When Elmore Torn was to return to Saigon, his friends the lepers took him through Vietcong road blocks in a crude coffin with air holes punched in it.

One Vietcong officer at a roadblock punched a stick into a hole in the coffin.

"He poked me in the belly and it really hurt but I managed to keep quiet, and I was carried on through the road-block by my friends the black-eye-loving lepers," said Mr. Torn.

It was not until he'd returned from Vietnam that Torn learned there was a rival organization to his National Black-eyed Pea Appreciation Association. This is the Black-eyed Pea Society of America, based in Richmond, Virginia, and the society's long-time No. One pea is the syndicated Washington columnist James J. Kilpatrick.

Mr.Kilpatrick also announced his awareness of Torn's group in this manner:

"Just one year ago this month [he was speaking in September of 1966], 300 lovers of the black-eyed pea gathered in the John Marshall [a Richmond, Virginia, hotel] and amidst the heavenly aroma of black-eyed peas and cornbread, the Black-eyed Pea Society of America sprang into being.

"In the gentlest possible way, Mr. Tolbert now advises me that this was a phoenix out of ashes. We are like Avis, the rent-a-car people. We are only No. 2. Many years ago a statesmen and a philosopher, Elmore Rural Torn of Taylor, Texas, founded the National Black-eyed Pea Appreciation Society, which now has thousands of members. Yet the news of this prestigious organization never reached us in Richmond until now. Truly we are not yet of the mainstream."

Torn replied to Kilpatrick: "Any friend of the black-eyed pea is a friend of mine. Perhaps our organizations can merge."

To which Kilpatrick responded: "Helping us through this difficult time is the generous attitude of Mr. Torn, who is exhibiting that nobility of spirit which identifies every lover of the black-eyed pea; he has welcomed our Virginia tendril to his long-established pea patch."

However, James J. Kilpatrick did scold Torn for being

ignorant of the life and literary works of the patron saint of the Virginia black-eyed pea lovers, a Dr. George W. Bagby, who wrote more than a century ago:

"Black-eye pea! Blessed black-eye! Sublime pellet! Celestial molecule! Divine little gob! All that Virginia is or has been or can be is owned to thee!"

Dr. Bagby in his mid-nineteenth-century essay said the black-eyed pea "is found in a curved, bumpy pod, three of which if straightened out would be about as long as the leading editorial in the Richmond *Whig* [an early newspaper]. The outside of this pod is a little rough, resembling green velvet, and the inside is lined with a white vegetable satin. In this sumptuous bed of the interior repose a half dozen or so of the blessed globules." Kilpatrick said that Dr. Bagby believed the black-eyed pea contained the very essence of Virginia, "and the more peas a person ate the better a Virginian he or she emerged. Whenever there is a deficiency of peas, or a neglect of the crop, just there the pernicious traits of northern character creep in . . ."

Coke Stevenson, a former governor of Texas who now ranches on the South Llano in the hill country, has a final chore every night before he goes to bed. Governor Stevenson puts some pinto beans in a pan of water to soak overnight. He rises around 4 A.M. and one of his first morning chores is to put the beans to simmering on the stove.

Range cooks such as Chalma Reid, Blondie Young, and Cap Warren have followed this same routine all their careers. For on the ranches of the Southwest, frijoles, usually boiled pinto beans, are served at both noon and evening meals.

Before you put them on to soak, clean the pintos through at least two waters and search for pebbles. The standard recipe calls for a cube of salt pork about one and a half inches in diameter with each pound of beans. The beans will expand wonderfully, and after they are well soaked, a few hours of boiling will cook them thoroughly.

You add salt to taste, and some range cooks mash up fresh

or dried chilipiquines and boil them with the beans — one tiny pepper for each serving would be piquant enough for a starter. Most ranchers, though, like their chilipiquines on the side, say about three to a serving, and mashed up in raw, sliced onions.

In a letter to Jane Trahey and Marihelen McDuff, who were editing a Neiman-Marcus cookbook called *A Taste of Texas,* the late J. Frank Dobie wrote:

"A meat eater could live on frijoles and never miss meat. When a Mexican laborer is unable to lift a heavy weight, his companions say he 'lacks frijoles.' As you may deduce, I am a kind of frijole man. On the old-time ranches of the border country, where I grew up, frijoles were about as regular as bread and in some households they still are. I like to eat one plate of beans, cooked with salt pork, and with the chilipiquines and raw onions, perhaps with a little vinegar, on the side for the main course, and honey-flavored pintos for dessert."

For "honey beans," omit the salt pork and season the pintos with two or three tablespoons of honey and a half teaspoon of salt for each pound of beans. These are also cooked until tender and served with hot corn bread, buttered, and covered with more honey.

17. Some Really "Hot" Bread

"We like even hotter peppers [than jalapeños], and fresh ones, to make our sauces."

Eva Rangel
on Mexican tastes

Through my daily column in the Dallas *News,* I was responsible for a revival of an old border recipe, jalapeño corn bread.

If you follow the directions of Mrs. Minnie E. Bell of El Paso, this almost amounts to a main dish.

The ingredients are: 3 cups of corn bread mix; 2½ cups of milk; ½ cup of salad oil; 3 beaten eggs; 1 large grated onion; 3 tablespoons of sugar; 1 cup of canned cream-style corn; ½ cup of pickled canned jalapeño peppers chopped very fine (if you want the bread more pungent use 1 twelve-ounce can of jalapeños); 1½ cups of grated yellow cheese; 2 ounces of chopped crisp bacon; ½ cup of finely chopped pimento peppers; and fresh mashed garlic or garlic powder to suit your tolerance of this.

You mix it all well and bake at 400° F. until done and brown.

Jalapeños, pickled or preserved in oil and vinegar, and usually with some diced carrots mixed in, are sold generally in the United States. But Mrs. Eva Rangel, of the City of Mexico, says jalapeños aren't the most popular hot peppers, by any means, in Mexico.

"We like even hotter peppers and fresh ones to make our sauces," said the beautiful Mrs. Rangel. Still, she confesses to a fondness for "this Texas recipe of yours," jalapeño corn bread, and she has begun to serve it at parties.

Mrs. Irene Martinez Garcia, one of the proprietors of the El Fenix chain of Mexican restaurants in Texas, said that my columns on jalapeño corn bread inspired her to do something never done in Mexico, as far as she knows, that is to mix hot chopped peppers, in this case jalapeños, in the tortilla dough.

Few readers of this book will be interested in making tortillas in the arduous, original way. With the introduction into American food stores of instant Masa Harina (corn meal made in the Indian way for tortillas and other breads), anyone can make this low-calorie bread on a *comal*, or griddle. Just follow the directions on the Masa Harina package as to how much water to add and how to knead the dough and shape the cakes.

At Mrs. Garcia's restaurant on Northwest Highway in Dallas, Mrs. San Juana Lopez is the tortilla maker, kneading the dough on a *metate* of volcanic rock. The *mano*, or roller, is made of the same hard, rough, porous rock. Mrs. Lopez, a stocky woman of pleasant countenance, works in a corner of the main hall of a complex of colorful rooms. (This particular restaurant looks like a palace of Spanish architecture and décor.)

The customers, especially children, are fascinated by San Juana's performance as she gracefully shapes the ball of tortilla dough into a thin, round, wide cake and then bakes it on the grill before her.

When *charro* musicians are playing in the room, San Juana

slaps out the cakes in rhythm with the violin and guitar. Then the children usually join in, clapping their hands in cadence with the movements of the tortilla artist.

Mrs. Lopez makes tortillas in "pepper calibers" from mild to hot. And they certainly go well with a real Mexican dish, such as *carne asada,* which consists of strips of tenderloin prime beef, with rice, guacamole, and the ubiquitous refried beans.

Personally, though, I wouldn't recommend either jalapeño corn bread or jalapeño tortillas with chili con carne or any other really highly flavored entree.

The blandness of a plain tortilla, crackers, or orthodox corn bread goes better, by contrast, with the pleasant sting of a bowl of red.

In Jefferson, Texas, the River Front Restaurant is presided over by Roy Butler, a former fighter pilot/soldier of fortune who barbecues meats Chinese-style, and his wife, Kay, a marvelous cook whose Alaskan-style sourdough bread is admirable.

The restaurant is in a former riverboat warehouse, a big brick building of Civil War or earlier vintage. Patrons sit at bare wooden tables on reed-bottom chairs of early Texas pattern. A huge barbecue pit in the rear serves as the cooking range. All broiling, baking, and even frying are done over hickory flames, and barbecued meats simmer in the smoke there for hours.

For an hors d'oeuvre, a small charcoal broiler is set in front of each customer and he can cook slices of country smoked sausage to his taste. With the sausage is served either coleslaw or delicately flavored salad of pickled green beans, pickled pinto beans and fresh lettuce, and there is also a plate of radishes, carrots, pickles, and hot peppers.

Ray Christopher of Brownfield, Texas, had a sourdough recipe which he worked out himself, mainly for biscuits. His directions for "quick starter" go like this: put 4 cups of warm water in a crock and stir in one package of powdered yeast. Add 2 cups of buttermilk, one tablespoon of sugar, 2 tablespoons of powdered (instant) potatoes, and enough flour to make a very thin batter. Leave this at room temperature 8 to 12 hours before time to make the biscuits. If you cover this container *never leave it airtight.* And never let this starter get older than 12 hours without adding a little sugar, as a good active starter is one secret for making good biscuits.

The simple biscuit-making operations go so: Sift 4 cups of flour and add 1 tablespoon of sugar, 1 teaspoon of salt (or more to suit your taste), ½ teaspoon of soda, 1½ teaspoons of baking powder.

Add ⅛ of a cup of shortening or margarine, not melted, and mix well. Stir the starter batter well, and mix in enough batter to make a soft dough — never make the dough too stiff. Roll out, cut, and place in a well-greased baking pan. Then set in a warm place and let the biscuits rise for 30 to 45 minutes. Then bake in a preheated oven at 450° to 475° F. Be sure to brush tops of biscuits with butter or margarine or shortening shortly before baking.

For thick, fluffy biscuits, leave dough about ¾ inch thick, then crowd biscuits into pan for better rising results. Use a cake pan at least 1½ inches deep, for a shallow pan will not allow rising.

My friend Rudolfo Hernández and I were in this little café in Matamoros, Mexico, across the river from Brownsville, one morning having a breakfast of coffee and mangos and crusty bread. Mexican bakers become poets with breadstuffs. I think Mexican *pan* equals or excels the best bread I've tasted in France.

And yet Rudy Hernández, a Mexican citizen, says that the most delicious bread he has ever eaten is the *pan de campo,* or camp bread, served by range *cocineros* on Texas' biggest cow spread, the 1,250,000-acre King Ranch. I know what he means. I've sampled King Ranch *pan de campo,* but it is no better than that served on many other ranches including Dolph Briscoe's cattle country on the Rio Grande near Catarina, Texas.

It was Easter time when Rudy and I were in the Matamoros café and some of the diners were having the traditional Easter dish, eggs scrambled with *nopalitos,* or the tender leaves of the young cactus.

Rudy wanted some *jicamina.* Only the café didn't have any that morning. The jicamina is a turnip-looking vegetable. Rudy said you cut off slivers and eat them in a lime juice or chili pepper sauce, and he touched fingers to his lips and then tossed a hand in the air to indicate his appreciation of the jicamina.

For some reason when you order a beer in many Mexican cafés along the Texas border you are served half a lime on the side, just as you are for *tequila con limón.*

18. Native Indian Foods and Farkleberries

"Our East Texas farkleberries certainly don't frizzle before they farkle."

Mrs. Ray Greene,
defending the local variety

A Kiowa Indian named Hunting Horse died in 1953 at the age of more than 110, his years being fairly well authenticated by reservation records. Hunting Horse rode on some of the last Kiowa raids on Texas and Mexico.

In 1952 I made my last of many visits with the proud old savage at his home in the Slick Hills of Oklahoma near Lawton. And, among other things, Hunting Horse told me that whites were very stupid in not recognizing the nutritional values of mesquite beans.

He said he owed his longevity in part to the fact that mesquite bean bread and cakes (the cakes flavored with honey and wild plums) were on his regular diet.

The only Tonkawa Indian I know, Roger (Rocky) Stallings, a San Antonio artist and sculptor and "resident Indian" at the University of Texas Institute of Texan Cultures at San Antonio, harvests mesquite beans in season and makes them into flour for bread and cakes, and into jellies and wines.

"I can make seven quarts of mesquite jelly out of about a gallon and a half of mesquite beans if I pound hell out of the beans," said the Tonkawa. "When they're ripe the beans are sweet and juicy, just packed with dextrose. You eat a log of mesquite bean jelly for breakfast and you won't get hungry until three o'clock in the afternoon and you're full of energy and raring to go. I would have liked to have known that old friend of yours, Hunting Horse. I bet that old scoundrel ate a lot of dry land terrapins and soft shell turtles. All the old time plains Indians did when they could get 'em, and I'm told turtle meat has a lot of vitamins including the rare Vitamin G in it."

Before he fries a steak (he prefers venison), Rocky rolls the meat in mesquite meal. "Gives a robust quality to the meat. Really cranks you up, because there are so many vitamins and good taste in mesquite meal," he says.

Before frying the steak, however, he pounds it, and between poundings works in some herbs, such as the chopped roots of young prairie onions and green leaves and seeds of rabbit peppers.

"A rabbit pepper, if you pick it when it is fresh and tender, has a flavor sort of like a fresh green pepper, only with a black pepper bite. You use only the roots of the wild prairie onion. It adds a magic flavor, just as does the rabbit pepper, to meat."

The trouble with Rocky's herb recipes is that you have to be something of a botanist and you have to search the prairies for ingredients such as rabbit peppers and wild onions. When he's doubtful about an herb, Mr. Stallings tries it on his pet ground squirrels and armadillos. "Anything an armadillo or a ground squirrel will eat is safe for a man to eat," said Rocky.

I'm not much of a wine connoisseur. Yet Rocky's mesquite

bean white is quite palatable and obviously of high alcohol content. It is a medium-sweet white liquid which he fortifies with a little honey.

At the Institute of Texan Cultures, the Tonkawa Indian is also resident "curandero," or "doctor" who uses native herbs. The staff members claim that a bad cough or an "I'm-about-to-have-the-flu" feeling can be relieved by drinking a Tonkawa tea made from the inner bark of mesquite boiled with sheep sorrel, leaves, and roots, tamarind, wild sage seeds, and a little honey. Rocky also claims that tea made from green pecan nuts will reduce fever.

Mr. Stallings was burning some dried plants which he identified as those of locoweed once when I visited his place out on the Floresville Road, south of San Antonio.

"Let locoweed smoke get in your eyes — just a little of it — and you'll have better vision, especially better night vision. In the old days Indians did this (they used a hide flume) before they went on night raids. It really works."

Rocky goes into the Texas Big Bend country regularly to get roots, sometimes weighing as much as twenty-five pounds, of the night-blooming cactus. The tuber acts as a storage compartment for liquids for the plant during dry weather. Rocky says that sap of this cactus root has some kind of pain-deadening effect: "I can soak my hands in it for a long time and then start handling hot coals. The juice when mixed with the soft pulp of *nopalitos* (tender cactus leaves) is a good dressing for wounds or sores. And dried pulp when burnt and mixed with the sap toughens scar tissue."

Rocky makes a tea of prickly ash or Hercules club root bark and some slivers off the trunk to ease sore throat pains. (Hercules club is sometimes called the toothache tree because of the pain-deadening power of its bark.) "One drink of this tea and you'll forget about your sore throat and start braying like a burro," said Rocky.

The Tonkawa herb doctor had some advice for women soon to birth babies: "About two weeks or so before a woman is due to domino, she should start eating boiled prairie turnips. This is an ancient Indian remedy for easing the pains of childbirth — and it really works. Don't eat the prairie turnip raw. Then it is as fiery as the hottest chili pepper, but it tames down considerably when boiled with a little side meat, and it is very tasty boiled — in a wild sort of way."

Rocky added: "Wild animals know about this. I've seen pregnant prairie dogs and pregnant thirteen-stripe ground squirrels devouring prairie turnips."

I asked an internationally renowned botanist, Dr. Donovan Correll of the National Science Foundation, about these wild turnips.

Dr. Correll said he believed that Stallings was talking about the large legumes of the *Psoralea* genus, enlarged round tubers at maturity called turnip root. These have brownish skins like Irish potatoes and are white when peeled, Dr. Correll said that the prairie turnips are ready for harvesting in November in Texas and are very prevalent in the Red River country, especially around Quanah, Texas.

"However, I know pastures around Fort Worth where you can gather them by the bushel. I've seen Indians eat them. I have never witnessed a pregnant prairie dog or ground squirrel eating a prairie turnip, though."

Rocky claims that tender cactus pads are among the most versatile of vegetables once you scrape away the spines. "I can prepare them more ways than a farmer can whip a mule," he said.

In the spring the yucca comes forth with waxy white flowers with many thick, juicy petals.

"The petals are what you eat," said Rocky. "Don't use the stem in the center of the flower, though. It's bitter. Even after taking out the stem and washing off the yellow pollen, the petals could cook a trace bitter. So I avoid this by throwing in a little sheep's sorrel. I parboil the petals just like okra and throw away the water. Cook them until tender, perhaps with some seasoning such as bacon or pork drippings.''

Stallings also makes excellent sauerkraut from yucca petals. Tastes pretty much as if it were made from cabbage.

Rock Stallings is attempting to organize something called the Original American Medical Association. The idea is for all the medicine men to organize. W. W. (Bill) Keeler, principal chief of the Cherokee nation and one of Rocky's acquaintances, seems to be enthusiastic about the proposed OAMA. Chief Keeler (who is also chairman of the board of Phillips Petroleum) said that all the medicine men should hold an annual convention where they would exchange information on herbs.

"People plow, bulldoze, burn up or just ignore some of the most precious of growing things," said Rocky, descendant of the Tonkawas, the tribe which once dominated the Texas hill country.

Between Looneyville and Cushing on a red clay log road in the hilly pine forests of northern Nacogdoches County, I talked with an elderly black man who had his mule-drawn wagon parked against the fence line, and he was baiting a small steel trap on a fence post with grains of corn.

"What kind of varmints do you catch on top of a fence post with corn bait?" I asked.

"Don't tell the game warden on me but I hope to catch me a crow or a young hawk," he responded, "and I hope they is frying-sized. I catch more crows and hawks in traps than I do shooting them."

I told him I was puzzled over his reference to frying-sized crows and hawks. And he said: "In olden days when hard times came we took to eating crows and hawks because we couldn't afford no other kind of meat. And we took a liking to them. They ain't nothing better than a young crow unless it's a fried young hawk."

Another authority I spoke with was Mrs. Sang-a-Lang Kerr, an elderly black who lived near the pleasant village of

Rural Shade, Navarro County. Mrs. Kerr said:

"I've eaten some crow, but no hawk. My brother, Ellis Rhynes, who passed two years ago, was mighty fond of fried young hawk. Just like quail, he said. They would be less sickness if folks ate more wild game. It was a fellow who used to run around with my brother, Ellis Rhynes, and this man was a Mexican. And he ate ho-ho owls."

In 1971 botanists discovered that Texas has the largest farkleberry tree in the United States, and possibly the largest in the world. (The king of all farkles is in Angelina County, near Zavalla, Texas, and the tree is twenty-nine feet high, forty inches in diameter, and has a spread of thirty-seven feet.)

The farkleberry (*Vaccinium arboreum marsh*) is a decorative blueberry also called sparkleberry or winter huckleberry, which "grows in sandy soils in pinelands, open mixed forests, thickets, clearings, fields, and coastal shrub forests from Florida to Texas and also north to Oklahoma, Indiana, Illinois, Missouri and Virginia."

That's what the botanical textbooks say on the farkleberry, so I was somewhat suspicious of an article in a Denver *Post* column by a fellow named Red Fenwick who claims there is an annual Farkleberry Festival in the hamlet of Hayti, South Dakota.

The fruit of the farkleberry is a subject of controversy. One distinguished botanist, while not saying that farkleberries aren't palatable, declared: "I've never known anyone who eats farkleberries."

East Texans disagree, although they say it's rather difficult to make jelly because the farkle fruit is so small, Mrs. Ray Greene of Gilmer, in East Texas, wrote me: "There is a patch of farkleberries at the gate of our farm. And my 12-year-old son, Russ, has developed quite a taste for farkleberries."

Arch Napier, an Albuquerque, New Mexico, writer who claims to be an authority on farkleberries, was another one who mentioned the annual Farkleberry Festival in Hayti, South Dakota, and he declares that "South Dakota farkleberries are more succulent than any others. Of course, any farkleberries anywhere are better than those in Texas and Florida. The summers are so hot in these unfortunate climes that the berries frizzle before they are fully farkled."

Mrs. Greene reacted angrily to Napier's statement: "Our East Texas farkleberries certainly don't frizzle before they farkle. I must admit that farkleberry muffins get mixed reviews from people to whom you serve them."

Mrs. Greene, one of the proprietors of the Gilmer newspaper, once wrote a beautifully worded essay on the fact that farkleberries, unlike some other eatable berries, cling to the branches and sustain birds throughout the cold months when food is scarce: "The scissor-tailed flycatchers have stripped persimmon trees of their sugar plum fruit and fox and possum grapevine vines have long since been denuded, and robins and bluebirds are making last inroads on the French mulberries and dogwood trees that still retain fruit, and crows have taken the last unguarded pecans. But all is not bleak for the small creatures because the farkleberries remain . . . ."

It is said that some East Texans distill a farkleberry brandy, but I've never encountered this liquor. In Arkansas the farkleberry is usually a bush or very small tree, yet it is revered. A book about Orval Faubus, a governor of Arkansas for many years, is called *All Around the Farkleberry Bush.* The author, George Fisher, speaks of "the awesome nutritional power of farkleberries."

A gag writer for the weekly television show called "Laugh-In" told me that he got the idea for the show's 'Farkle Family' from reading one of my Dallas *News* columns years ago in praise of the farkleberry.

An early day Harvard-type botanist, Dr. Charles Sprague Sargent, in his book *Manual of the Trees of North America,* claimed he discovered a farkleberry tree in East Texas which was ten feet in diameter. (He must have had too much East Texas white lightning when he wrote the section on far-kleberries in his book.)

Dr. Sargent was right when he said that Texas farkleber-ries ripen in October and the berries are "slightly astringent, the flesh of pleasant flavor." He then takes on the role of herb doctor when he says that "decoctions of the astringent bark of the farkleberry roots and the leaves are useful in the treatment of dysentery." He said that the closely grained wood of the farkleberry is very good for making hoe handles, police billy clubs, and the bark is sometimes used by tanners.

Mrs. A. D. Lemons of Henderson, Texas, says that far-kleberries make the very best jelly in the world. "Only trouble is that it takes the patience of Job and more free time than most people have to collect enough of the tiny berries to make just one glass of jelly. If you have the time it is well worth the effort."

Hopkins County, of which Sulphur Springs is the county seat, has been famous for a century or more for a stew in which squirrels furnished the main ingredient. Nowadays Hopkins County stew is made mostly with chicken as the meat base. In 1971 the county had a stew cookoff and Mr. and Mrs. Herman Burkham of Dike, Hopkins County, were the winners. These are the ingredients for their winning formula: 3 pounds of cut-up chicken, 1 pound of beef tallow, 2 cans of yellow cream-style corn, 2 cans of tomatoes, 2 pounds of diced white potatoes, 2 pounds of diced Bermuda onions, 2 level tablespoons of sugar, 3 level tablespoons of chili powder, 1 level teaspoon of cayenne pepper, 2 ta-blespoons of salt.

You combine everything except the corn with one quart of water and cook for 2 hours at a very slow boil. If more water is needed make it hot water. After the 2-hour period add the corn and simmer for 5 minutes more. The beef tallow is only for flavor, and lift it out before serving. This makes 2 gallons of stew.

Alas, the Catfish Inn in Rio Grande City has closed. It was the only café I know about which served "broiled crotalus." Crotalus is the polite and scientific name for rattlesnake meat.

"Doesn't anyone around here serve crotalus any more?" I asked George Reynold Boyle, proprietor of Hotel Ringgold, which is across Laredo Street from the site of the old Catfish Inn.

"Well, I always have a good supply in my refrigerator for serving at cocktail parties," said Mr. Boyle. "I've no restaurant in my hotel but I serve crotalus a la Boyle as an hors d'oeurvre when geologists hold regional or state meetings here." (The scene for these cocktail parties is under the banana trees and palms in the hotel's courtyard garden.)

Mr. Boyle is a Harvard graduate, a geologist, and a gourmet cook who found the warm Rio Grande climate to his liking. He has his geologist's office in the little hotel, and in this office is a card file of more than two thousand recipes, some of them for quite exotic dishes, which he collected while working all over the world.

"My rancher friends bring me in freshly killed rattlers," said George Boyle. "The way I prepare it, marinated in citrus juice and black pepper and nutmeg for three hours and then sautéed in butter, rattlesnake meat is delicious and has the texture of scallops. The hardest thing is getting someone to take the first bite. So in inviting a guest to try it I just say, 'Have some crotalus!' Once tried it is appreciated under any name."

This is the procedure for preparing "crotalus a la Boyle": "Remove head and skin. Clean the meat and cut into 2-inch-long pieces and marinate for 3 hours in, preferably, the juice of sour oranges (which grow in these regions of the Lower Rio Grande) or in sweet orange juice acidulated with lemon juice, along with peppercorns and a dash of nutmeg, to suit your taste. Then drain the meat and wipe the pieces clean. Sprinkle lightly with salt. Dip in beaten egg and roll in fine bread crumbs. Sauté meat in hot butter until pieces are brown. That's it."

19. A Land of Hot Sausage and Barbecue

*"There is simply nothing better than **chivos** if properly barbecued."*

Tony (The Fox) Zapata,
premier goat-barbecuing artist

Colonies of Germans, Poles, and Czechs came to Texas in the nineteenth century. There were not only superlative farmers and stock raisers among them, there were also craftsmen, artisans, mechanics, schoolteachers, scientists.

Some arrived in the years of the Republic of Texas (1836-45), or earlier. Some came under titled leaders, such as the German Prince Karl of Solms-Braunfels, who founded the delightfully Teutonic Texas town of New Braunfels, or Baron von Meusebach and his wife, the Countess of Tyrol, whose creation, Fredericksburg, hub up now to the LBJ Ranch, was the hometown of Admiral Chester Nimitz.

The food became a delicious blending of the Old World and the New.

There is a gastronomic rivalry between some of these

towns. For instance, New Braunfels and Castroville, also near San Antonio, have a continuous "wurst war."

Since the days of Prince Karl, New Braunfels has prided itself on its sausage makers. The town on the mighty Comal Springs has an annual six-day celebration called Sausage Week. New Braunfels calls itself "The Sausage Capital of the Southwest." This title has been challenged by Castroville, founded in 1844 by colonists mostly from Alsace, under Count Henri de Castro.

Joe L. Schott, descendant of the first Alsatian families and editor of the *Castroville Bulletin,* started the "wurst war" with this editorial: "New Braunfels has 17,000 population and produces about 300,000 pounds of sausage annually. Castroville has only about 1,800 people and yet we produce 266,000 pounds of sausage every year, and this doesn't count around 4,000 pounds consumed at each Festival of St. Louis here in August."

Editor Schott figured that, on a per capita basis, his townsmen are the sausage-making champions. He also wrote: "They make some mighty fine sausage in New Braunfels and yet it doesn't compare in flavor and texture with that composed by just three butcher shops in Castroville. Alsatians are partly French and they put some delicate flavors in sausage with which a German sausage maker would never bother."

Dr. Edgar A. Grist, chairman of Sausage Week at New Braunfels, simply replied to editor Schott this way: "New Braunfels will always make more and better sausage than Castroville."

The Smokehouse in New Braunfels is an exception, but, for some reason, really good restaurants are few in the "German," "Polish," and "Czech" counties of Texas. The cooking just doesn't match that in the homes, anyway.

If you want to get some really good sausage in Castroville, for instance, you would go to the butcher shops of Dan Burrell, or Fred and Thomas Boubel, or to Butsy Beck's Smokehouse. (Butsy Beck smokes the best beef jerky I've ever tasted.)

In fact, in these towns where there are many folk of German, Polish, or Czech ancestry, the best places to eat are often in the smoky back rooms of meat markets.

The furnishing back of the butcher shop will probably consist only of benches and crude tables. Chained to the tables will be sharp butcher knives, the only table utensils.

Part of the back room will likely be taken up by a small sausage factory. There will always be a big brick barbecue pit over which beef, mutton, goat meat, and sausages will cook for hours, very slowly, from smoke as much as heat radiation. The pits will be fueled with hickory, oak, or mesquite.

You'll get your serving of meat (a big link of hot sausage for about twenty-five cents) on butcher's wrapping paper, along with pickles, sliced Bermuda onions, and crackers — they seldom serve bread in these places. Texas-brewed beer will be twenty-five cents or less a bottle.

There may be a babble of language, with Spanish, German, Czech, and Polish heard as well as English. Many Texans in these counties speak two, three, and four languages.

Krause's Grocery and Market in Lockhart, south of Austin, is a good example of such places. The smoked sausage plant and the huge brick barbecue pits and the serving rooms have crowded the grocery store and the meat market into a corner of the first floor of the nineteenth-century, two-story brick building. Another famous barbecue establishment in Lockhart is Black's, which long ago dispensed with its meat market and became just an informal café.

Taylor, Texas, northeast of Austin, has more barbecue places, all of them featuring hot, smoked German or Polish sausage, than any town of ten thousand that I know about. Probably the best is a spot where the sign reads simply, "Louie Mueller's — Hot Sausage," although you can get all kinds of barbecued meat there, including a sizable T-bone steak with pickles, onions, and crackers, for $1.25, or around that.

In towns such as Pflugerville, also near Austin, and Blieblerville, south of Brenham, there are saloon-like eating places where you can get excellent and inexpensive barbecue, and these connect with general stores or meat markets, although not in the back rooms.

East Texas' most memorable barbecue artists are (or were) blacks. I used to go to bird dog field trials near Palestine, Texas, and we made our headquarters at Dr. Gee's General Store in the village of Bethel. The barbecue cook at these field trials was a tall, intelligent, dedicated old black whose full name was King Solomon.

King Solomon would work all night over his coals before a field trial, cursing the bird dogs, for he claimed that the barking and howling of many dogs would cause bad weather. He believed that his success at barbecuing rested heavily on his "secret devil's sauce," and he wouldn't tell anyone, not even his family, the formula, although some of the ingredients were, obviously, fresh chili pepper sauce, Worcestershire sauce (King Solomon said he made his own Worcestershire), black pepper, and vinegar. It was very hot.

Johnnie Brown, a heavy-set, cheerful black who cooks for hunting parties around Wills Point, Texas, told me that he was heavily burdened with his own "devil's sauce recipe." Johnnie Brown explained:

"I got a worry with me all the time. About fifteen years ago, Lank Robinson give me the receipt for his barbecue sauce, and it is the best devil's sauce they is. Lank Robinson was a real barbecuing man. He could cook sweeter over red oak than anyone else can over hickory.

"He made me swear not to tell what's in that sauce until I'm just about to die. What worries me is how am I going to know when I'm just about to die?"

A surprising number of the barbecue artists in Dallas come from an East Texas hamlet in Wood County called Mutt-and-Jeff. Mutt-and-Jeff was so titled many years ago because the contrasting physical dimensions of the village's two leading merchants suggested the tall and short characters in the cartoon strip *Mutt and Jeff.*

In the olden days, Mutt-and-Jeff was famous for barbecue. In 1926, one of the leading barbecue men, R. O. Shoemaker, moved to Dallas and opened a barbecue stand. This stand blossomed into a chain of stands. Later, two of R. O. Shoemaker's brothers and many of his friends and relatives followed him to Dallas. They either went to work in a Shoemaker stand or opened their own places.

Now, the chances are very good that the next time you order a barbecue sandwich in Dallas, especially in the downtown section, the man who cooked the beef, pork, or sausage for the sandwich is a native of Mutt-and-Jeff.

The most talented barbecue man I know along the Texas-Mexico border is Antonio (The Fox) Zapata, who lives in Judge Roy Bean's old seat for "The Law West of the Pecos," Langtry, Texas.

In Langtry, by a deep, technicolor gorge of the Rio Grande, Mr. Zapata is also the waterworks superintendent, the plumber, photographer, school bus driver, butcher, and barber. (In his barbershop, with its walls of heavy railroad crossties, the building dating back to the days of Judge Roy Bean, Mr. Zapata has a short interview with a customer before he performs the haircut. The haircut has to be "contracted" for on a sliding scale of prices. For example, The Fox will cut the hair of a nearly bald man for, say, fifty cents while he may charge $2.50 for the same service to a sheepherder who hasn't had a haircut in six months and has burrs in his mane.)

Tony Zapata goes back to the days when a whole beef was simply gutted and barbecued *con cuero,* that is, with the hide and hair left on the carcass. The hide would seal in the natural juices during the twenty-four-hour or more cooking process in a closed pit over mesquite coals.

Nowadays, Tony Zapata's favorite subjects for barbecuing

are *chivos,* or yearling goats. "There is simply nothing better than *chivos* if properly barbecued," declared Mr. Zapata. "Barbecued beef can't compare with *chivos.*" Many folks along the Rio Grande agree.

The cooking process is simple. The yearling goats are split down the middle, impaled on an iron cross from four to six feet over a good fire of mesquite coals, and cooked for hours, or until well done.

A Texas Tech professor told me: "I don't think you're going to get too far in your current search for good, inexpensive eating places in Texas. Most Texas restaurants, even the more expensive ones, are still mediocre, just as George Sessions Perry said they were in a 1942 book."

I told the prof (a third-generation Texan) that parts of Texas, especially the small towns in the northwestern reaches of the state, are still almost wildernesses as far as the quality of the food produced in the café is concerned. In the big Texas cities I think the restaurants have "caught up" with the rest of the nation.

George Sessions Perry was a Texas novelist who spent a lot of time in Connecticut exile. In his 1942 book he wrote thus on Texas café food: "It is said that in frontier days the frying pan killed more settlers than did the Indians. But that is because the frying pan had no competition from the present-day small town Texas café plate lunch. Otherwise, the honors would have been differently distributed . . ."

Mr. Perry then delivered a rhetorical attack on the ubiquitous entree on most small-town Texas menus: the chicken-fried steak. Now, personally, I think this can be a delight when prepared from veal or a yearling steak. I've known some chuck wagon cooks who could do wonders with veal. And the great artist at chicken-fried steak of my childhood was Shorty Thornton, who ran a paper napkin café in Littlefield, Texas.

On the chicken-fried steak, Perry wrote: "The fried steak

is a tough, greasy mess that only a famished hound would relish. In addition, you get a dollop of boiled navy beans, a cud of greasy turnip greens . . . The best thing in most small town restaurants is the pot of chili con carne they keep simmering on the back stove . . ."

It must be mentioned that Mr. Perry knew little about the culinary situation in the hill country and in West Texas in 1942. And he was violently prejudiced against Mexican cooks and Mexican cookery.

In Ciudad, Acuña, Mexico, across the Rio Grande from Del Rio, Texas, I talked with a *menudero,* or dealer in tripe. There on a busy sidewalk he also had a tripe stew, called *menudo,* simmering in a big pot on a portable stove fed with mesquite knots.

The menudero was quite a salesman. In Tex-Mex, the border lingo of Spanish and Texanese, he proclaimed that one bowl of menudo would cure my hangover.

"But I don't suffer from a hangover," I said.

"Perhaps, you will very soon, señor," he predicted. "My menudo also prevent the hangover."

I wasn't in the mood for any sidewalk menudo.

The next day, though, in a Mexican food restaurant in Helotes (meaning green corn) in the Texas hill country, I did sample some menudo.

This was prepared by a nice woman named Mrs. Andrea Morelos. She has a modern kitchen in her Helotes restaurant — yet she cooks the menudo outside in a big iron pot over a hickory or mesquite fire. "For some reason menudo doesn't really taste like menudo to me unless it is cooked over a wood fire." she said.

The tripe, or lining of a cow's stomach, is diced like chili meat. Then the "honeycomb," as Mrs. Morelos calls tripe, is cooked with hominy and chili peppers (or chili powder if the chilies aren't available).

She said that menudo is an ideal entree for people with stomach complaints. "One man who comes to my place for menudo, a big doctor from Galveston with diamond rings all over his fingers, thinks menudo is a cure for stomach ulcers," said Mrs. Morelos.

I found her version of menudo quite tasty. And it gives the tummy a warm feeling.

In Castroville, Butsy Beck makes grand-tasting jerky, or rather the Alsatian version of jerked beef. According to Butsy's directions you take a hunk of lean beef — all the fat must be removed or it becomes rancid in a hurry — and soak it overnight in a brine so heavy an egg will float in it. A weight is used to keep the beef under the salt water. Next you use a sacking needle to make a hole through the piece of beef and attach a string through the beef. Then boil the beef in unsalted water until the meat turns white.

The cooked beef is then rolled in coarse-ground black pepper; completely cover the meat with black pepper, and then hang the beef in a smokehouse. Busty Beck uses mesquite wood in the smokehouse. When he has bright mesquite coals he throws damp hickory sawdust on the coals and gets a lot of smoke. He keeps the meat in the smokehouse for three days, giving the meat an hour of "good smoking," using fans to help dry it out each of the three days. Then it's ready.

"Breakfast at Cisco's" has a magic meaning to many people, including Lyndon Johnson. Cisco's is in a nineteenth-century, red brick, two-story building at 1411 East Sixth Street in Austin, Texas.

One sign outside reads "Cisco's Bakery," and this *is* a real Mexican-style bakery producing many pastries and what might be called French loaves only they are styled "bolillos" at Cisco's. Another marquee outside indicates a café. It is decorated with a good caricature of the proprietor, Rudy (Cisco) Cisneros and recites that Cisco's features "the internationally famous maitre d', El Mosco."

Rudy Cisneros and El Mosco are personalities who complement the food and atmosphere at Cisco's. So do Rafael

Martínez, the baker, who is from San Luis Potosí, Mexico, and an anonymous woman who makes delightful tamales in her home for the café.

"Why is the name of the genius who makes your hot tamales a secret?" I asked Mr. Cisneros.

The answer revolves around the fact that Lyndon Johnson bought tamales for several decades at Cisco's. And sometimes you could catch LBJ there at breakfast or at one of the every Wednesday meetings of an organization called the Gavalle Gardenia Luncheon Club.

After he became President, Mr. Johnson continued to order tamales from Cisco's. Only then Secret Service men had to visit the tamale woman's home and check on her background and on sanitary conditions in her kitchen. She passed inspection. Yet the visit of the Secret Service so perturbed her that she asked Rudy that her name never appear again in public print.

The sweet rolls are good, and some of the other breakfast fare includes *huevos rancheros* and Mexican sausage with, of course, hot bolillos, and French fried potatoes always prepared fresh, and refried beans. Tortillas are made on a stone grill. And for luncheon there is "country style" Mexican food such as you might be served on a rancho. *The Chuck Wagon*, magazine of Texas restaurant people, once called Cisco's "a Brook Farm for the press and politicians . . . East Austin residents (most of Latin descent) feel equally at home." The Gavalle Gardenia Luncheon Club (the café and bakery are in what was formerly an Austin suburb called Gavalle) started as a women's luncheon club, but gradually male politicos and newspapermen have taken over.

El Mosco or "The Fly" is so called because the maitre d' has "beeg LBJ-type ears" and looks as if he's ready to fly away. He is a native of Matamoros, Mexico, who has been a fixture at Cisco's for about fourteen years.

I asked The Fly why the sign outside proclaims him an internationally famous maitre d'.

"I guess it mean I do everything right," said El Mosco, modestly.

Incidentally, Cisco's tamale woman still fills orders to be sent by air to dozens of customers in Washington, D.C., who acquired tastes for "White House Tamales" while LBJ was in office.

Most of these customers are congressmen. She says that she usually makes the tamale mildly spiced for patrons from Northern states "while they are really hot for members of the Texas delegation."

J. R. McClellan, of Dallas' Spanish Village Restaurant, thinks that *mole* is the most gourmet-ish of all Mexican cookery. He doesn't serve mole in his excellent café, yet here are his instructions for making it:

"The ingredients are 1 quart of chicken stock, 2 tablespoons of flour, ½ cup of ajonjolí (sesame seeds), 2 heaping tablespoons of chili powder, 4 squares of Mexican chocolate, 1 rounded teaspoon of cinnamon, 2 bay leaves. Combine and blend all the ingredients except the cinnamon and bay leaves. Stir frequently and bring to a good boil until thickened. Remove from heat and add cinnamon and bay leaves. Serve over broiled spring chicken or sliced breast of roasted chicken.

This sounds easy and it is except for the ajonjolí. To prepare the ajonjolí you cook 1 cup of sesame seeds over a slow fire in a small iron skillet. Use no oil because sesame seeds have enough oil to provide for themselves. Stir the seeds constantly and cook for about 15 minutes or until they take on a nice tan color. Then put the seeds on a Mexican metate and grind into a smooth paste. The metate must be placed on the floor and the operator must be in a kneeling position over it.

"There is no other way and this is pure hell to do. But once you do it you have a delicately flavored paste that adds magic to the mole. In fact, it isn't mole if it doesn't have ajonjolí."

Why doesn't he serve mole in his restaurant? Well, most of his customers seem to be pepper-pod-loving peasants such as Tolbert. "There doesn't seem to be any demand for mole around here," said J. R.

Some of the most gourmet-ish meals in Texas are prepared and served in a highly unlikely place, the Hill Top Herb Farm on the Hill Store Road in San Jacinto County, south of the town of Cold Spring. The proprietor and cook, Mrs. Madalene Hill, known as "The Yarb Woman" to her Piney Woods neighbors, requires reservations: "I wouldn't serve the Queen of England without a reservation. I'm not running a short order café. These meals have to be carefully prepared."

You'd better not be pressed for time if you dine at the herb farm, for these are complete meals from soup to nuts, and with the accent on the flavors of herbs. For samples, you may find the luscious hearts of geraniums or dandelion greens in your salad, and the dressing may be composed in part of Forty Thieves Vinegar, this being vinegar containing forty taste-haunting herbs.

The Hill Top Herb Farm ships green leaf herbs air freight all over the world. Besides culinary and decorative herbs, medicinal herbs are also raised for customers as far away as a medical college in Padua, Italy. More than three hundred varieties of herbs are grown on thirteen acres.

"A visit to our hilltop isn't just a visit to an herb farm but rather a day to be spent communing with God's work," said Mrs. Hill.

You can buy excellent German-style smoked meats in Austin County, Texas, markets and even in the many roadside beer taverns. I was surprised to find, though, that chicken stew, prepared about like the famous Hopkins County version, is the favored entree at parties in villages such as Welcome, Industry, New Ulm, Raccoon Bend, Frydek, and Cat Spring.

For many years the most admired chicken stew cook in the county was the late Charley Strauss of Bellville, a relative of Fritz Strauss, the Cat Spring barber who still charges fifty cents for a haircut.

Until 1972, Charley Strauss's heir as the chicken stew cooking champion of Austin County was Ellis Jones, also of Bellville, a slender, quick-witted black man who said he "put in about 150 years cooking for people around here."

Unfortunately for the gastronomical good of the county, Ellis Jones has retired, inserting the following notice in Franz Zeiske's Bellville *Times,* thanking the people for whom he has toiled over the stewpot:

"I, Ellis Jones, am now retiring after cooking for the following: Mr. Eddie Koerth for 40 years, Lawyer Ennis Hill for 41 years, the late Dr. Steck for 31 years, the late Mr. Max Bader for 10 years, the county for 10 years or more, the Sante Fe Railroad for 10 years, Dr. H. E. Roensch for 5 years, etc., etc. . . . On special occasions I served as cook for parties, camps, churches, and hunters. During these many years I have never been fired from a job. I've always tried to do my best. I am thankful to God, and for those who have helped me thus far. My wife, Grace, and I are at our home on West Austin Street. Thanks to all . . ."

In Texas towns where the majority of the citizens are of Czech descent, a girl's popularity is gauged by the number of kegs of beer served at her after-the-wedding supper.

In Praha, Fayette County, and Zabcikville, Bell County, and West, McLennan County, I talked with many women who'd had "eight-keg weddings."

In Nemicek's sausage and smoked bacon emporium in West, Emil Nors said: "We've had some ten-keg weddings."

"I remember several twelve-keg weddings," said Johnny Hornak. "Someday a girl here will have a fourteen-keg wedding and her name will go down in history."

Clarendon, in the Texas Panhandle, was named for either

the wife of the town's founder, Mrs. Clara Carhart, or for the British Earl of Clarendon. (In the last two decades of the nineteenth century, Clarendon town was in a nest of great ranches owned by members of the British nobility.)

The founder was a Methodist preacher. And in the old days the rowdy cowboys of the area referred to Clarendon as "The Saints' Roost" because the early colonizers of the town were against whiskey drinking, wenching, and other sports favored by the cowhands.

The early Clarendon women were famous cooks. And in 1972 the town's fine culinary tradition was personified in an eating place called Mrs. Bromley's Fine Foods. This is one of those out-of-the-way restaurants which, on merit and some salesmanship on the part of the proprietor, winds up getting big spreads in national women's magazines and in such publications as *Ford Times.*

Mrs. Ruby Bromley's café is in an old-fashioned story-and-a-half house of the architectural scheme known in the 1920s as an "airplane bungalow."

When I made my latest visit to Mrs. Bromley's Fine Foods, the place was crowded with cattlemen in Clarendon for a livestock sale.

You take a table at the start and are served a huge bowl of homemade soup and a salad. Then you go down the buffet line, where on this day the entrees were marvelous roast of beef, pork chops, fried chicken, and ham. Previously you'd had a choice of five fresh salads. And on the buffet line there were seven or eight vegetables dishes and for dessert either cherry pecan cobbler or strawberry shortcake.

Mrs. Bromley, a cheerful, attractive woman, moves around the dining room cheering on the customers to go back for fresh helpings. On this particular day she welcomed the majority among her guests thus:

"It's always nice to have you cattle buyers and bull salesmen. Don't feel bashful about going back for seconds or thirds."

The hallway of the old house is literally papered with the business cards of appreciative travelers.

December is a time when the Bosque County countryside is at its handsomest. Then the sumac and other bright botany are flame-colored against the intense green, watercolor-like wash of the cedar jungles in these hills and mesas. And in December, Bosque County people start thinking about lutefisk.

Lutefisk means dried fish imported from Norway. An English-Norwegian dictionary defines lutefisk as "a codfish steeped in lye of potash."

Norwegian settlers first came to Bosque County in 1857 under the leadership of Cleeng Pearson, the "father" of Norse immigration to the U.S. and a man whose memory is much revered in Minnesota. Lutefisk is the holiday dish in Norway, especially around Christmas time, I was told.

Probably in 1857, when the Comanches and Kiowas were still scalping Bosque County inhabitants, the Norsemen had to do without their imported fish from the homeland. Ever since the railroads came, though, the people of Norwegian descent in Bosque County have been getting their shipments of lutefisk in time for dining during the holidays.

The town of Cranfills Gap in the county has been having an annual Lutefisk Festival for longer years than springs the memory of eighty-five-year-olds such as Sven Hanson.

In early December the lutefisk starts arriving from Norway, in bales stiff as planks and sometimes three feet long. Also in recent times lutefisk comes frozen, prepared in Norway. For many decades Cranfills Gap's stone St. Olaf's Lutheran Church sponsored the annual Lutefisk sometime in December. Now the local Lions Club runs the annual dinner, held now in the high-school cafeteria. As much as five hundred pounds of lutefisk is served at the dinner, although there's also turkey for those who've not acquired a taste for Norwegian codfish.

In order to prepare the dried fish, it is soaked in fresh water and lye of potash for two days. Then it is soaked in lime water for another two days. After that the fish is thoroughly rinsed, and it has begun to take on the appearance of freshly caught codfish. It has also become three or four times as big as when it arrived in the dried state.

The lutefisk is then boiled and served with a Norwegian-accented white sauce.

Ernest Lowery's newspaper advertisements for his café in Breckenridge, Texas, used to read: "The finest steaks in West Texas cooked as I want to cook them. No atmosphere. No pretty girls. Just good steaks and beer . . ."

The café is in an old frame building which hasn't been stroked by a paint brush in many a decade. There's a crude sign which reads: "Lowery's Steaks and Beer." That sign could also serve as the menu. He doesn't even bother with coffee, although he does serve a palatable tossed salad and French fries. If you want ice, Mr. Lowery will advise you to go to a nearby service station and store and buy your own ice.

The interior is most unpretentious: old tables and chairs, no tablecloths, paper napkins, and the dusty walls are decorated with Mr. Lowery's collection of more than 1,500 ball-point pens. (He won't explain why he collects ball-points.)

Ernest Lowery won't open his café on days when his feet hurt, or when he wants to go dancing at the Belvania — this being a "night club" which is also in operation during daylight hours.

His steaks are always T-bones, about two inches thick and weighing at least one pound. He refuses to charcoal broil a steak.

"I might consider charcoal if I could find the old-fashioned kind. But this stuff they sell for charcoal now seems to be made from old, wadded-up newspapers. I'll never cook a frozen steak, either. I think the flavor goes off in the ice. The reason some steaks wind up well done is that you have to broil a frozen steak well done to get the ice out of the middle," he said.

In the summertime Hempstead, Texas, has almost as many sidewalk cafés as Paris, France. Only in the Waller County capital, once called Six-Shooter Junction, the sidewalk cafés serve only slices of cold watermelon, and usually these establishments consist mainly of crude tables and chairs under canvas.

I asked one of the watermelon café operators, Roy Feagan, Jr., about this: "Hempstead must have one watermelon café for each hundred inhabitants. How do you folks make it? Selling sliced watermelon to one another?"

"Well, we're at the intersection of several highways," said Mr. Feagan, "and people who travel a lot get in the habit of stopping here. They appreciate the fact that Waller County raises the finest melons in the land.

"My father started the first watermelon sidewalk café here years ago. Now someone is ready to get another one going as soon as there's a vacant corner along the highways through town. Business is pretty good, too."

Mrs. Vivian Hartman, a friend to whose good taste I genuflect, introduced me to Ann King's "monkey bread." Ann King, a good-looking black women, long ago worked out her formula for monkey bread with the late film actress Zasu Pitts.

If you're a veteran viewer of movies you'll remember Zasu Pitts. She was the sweet-faced, willowy character actress with popping, bewildered eyes, and she was much given to anxiously wringing her hands when before the cameras. Miss Pitts was quite a gourmet and composed several cookbooks including one called *Candy Hits by Zasu Pitts*.

Mrs. King won't give her formula for monkey bread, but you can buy it most days at the Piggly-Wiggly store in Albany, Texas, where Ann lives.

At the store it comes frozen and in a one-pound ring,

shaped sort of like an angel food cake. You just brown and become an addict. The rolls of bread are all twisted up in spaghetti snarls. I like it rather well browned and it's so "short" you don't need any butter with it.

"I took out a patent on my version of monkey bread," said Ann King. "I understand some restaurant in Dallas is serving what they call monkey bread, but my customers say it doesn't taste nearly so good as mine."

Wilbur Salad is more of a hearty entree than a salad. It is the innovation of Doc Daniel, the now retired maestro of the Dallas *News* cafeteria. Doc named it in honor of a Dallas *News* editor of bygone days, Wilbur Keith.

The ingredients of Wilbur Salad are shredded lettuce, chopped fresh tomatoes, chopped-up Cheddar cheese (the stronger the better), chopped hard-boiled eggs, chopped-up crisp bacon. Over this you pour of little hot bacon grease and then mix it up.

The former White Elephant Saloon, now vacant, on Fredericksburg's main street was once famous for the quality of its free lunch. This old stone building has a New Orleans-like lacework of wrought iron out front, and over the door there is the stone likeness of a white elephant.

The White Elephant is owned by the Kurt Keidel family. Miss Margaret Keidel has done some research on the significance of the white elephant crest. She said that since the days of Hannibal's invasion of Europe with his elephant corps, a white elephant has signified a place where food and drink are served. Hannibal's army foraged off the country as they marched against the Romans, and at inns or at houses where the food pleased the Carthaginians, Hannibal caused the sign of the white elephant to be painted out front.

Green pecan wood a-burning in coals makes a light blue, sweet-smelling smoke. Should you drive into Fulshear, a village in Fort Bend County just east of Houston, the fragrance of pecan wood smoke is almost certain to grace the atmosphere, especially when you draw nigh to Ed Dozier's place, where a battery of smokehouses and barbecue pits are usually in operation.

"There's no hickory in these reaches of Fort Bend County. So we turned to green pecan wood, which, I think, is far superior to hickory for smoking meats and for barbecuing," said Mr. Dozier. In the nearby bottoms of the lower Brazos River and in Bessie's Creek there are jungles of pecans. And Mr. Dozier, who operates a meat market and barbecue café, said he sends out a truck about once a week "to thin out the pecans in the bottoms."

In the café section you can get barbecued brisket of beef or sausages. In the market section there are many smoked meats, such as Canadian bacon, bacon, what are called peppered ham slugs, hams, pork loins, smoked turkeys, and many varieties of sausage, all from the pecan-fired smokehouses.

And the jerky is outstanding. In Fort Bend County jerky is sometimes called "Dozier's chewing gum," and you need a healthy set of teeth to handle it. The jerky is the highest priced meat in the shop, mainly because after four days in the smokehouse five and a half pounds of fresh lean beef will be transformed into about a pound and a half of chewy, delightful jerky.

For some reason the hottest chilipiquines, or little wild chili peppers, seem to grow in Fort Bend County. Anyway, that's been my experience. If you doubt this, stop in Mrs. Julie Fails' little café in the hamlet of Didy Waw Didy, Fort Bend County, and sample some of her preserved wild peppers.

There's usually a pot of chili con carne simmering on the stove. And I asked Mr Fails if his wife included those powerful little wild peppers in her chili formula.

"Lord, no," said Mr. Fails. "School children here in and

around Didy Waw Didy and Juliff communities eat this chili. And they couldn't take the fire in these bird peppers."

In folklore, Didy Waw Didy (sometimes spelled Ditty Wah Ditty) was the last "stop" on a mythical railroad bound for hell. And there's an old song, made famous by Phil Harris, with the refrain:

> It ain't a town and it ain't a city —
> Just a little place called Didy Waw Didy!

In 1854 a group of colonists from Germany, led by a fellow named Ernst Herman Altgelt, settled on the spring-fed Guadalupe River in Kendall County, Texas. Herr Altgelt was said to be so charmed by what these pioneers called "The Hills of God" and the sparkling water that he said: "This should be a place of everlasting comfort." So the settlement was titled Camp Comfort, later shortened to Comfort.

Some of the best country-style cooking in the Texas hill country may be found today at the Cypress Creek Inn in Comfort.

The Cypress Creek Inn has been operated for more than twenty years by Mrs. Charlotte Holmes, who is the cook, and by her husband, Damon "Grandpa" Holmes. Mr. Holmes is maitre d', waiter, sometime bartender, and full-time comedian, an incredibly lively old boy of eighty-six.

Although this is a paper-napkin-type café, Grandpa Holmes often wears a high silk hat while serving the customers, who are often confused by the "reserved" signs on all vacant tables. Apparently these signs mean nothing, for veteran patrons ignore them. When the place gets nearly full, Damon Holmes usually locks the front door. Then the regular customers come in the back way.

The prices are amazingly low. For instance, there is the ninety-five-cent special consisting of two big slabs of delicious German-style smoked sausage, freshly cooked carrots which never saw a steam table, green salad with watercress in it, potatoes, and slabs of tart pie made from fresh Kendall County peaches (in season) between a memorable pastry.

In New Braunfels, another Texas "German town," settled in 1854 by colonists under Prince Carl of Solms-Braunfels, there's a good restaurant, although with New York City-style prices, called the Smokehouse. No restaurant, not even in Canada, can equal the Smokehouse's Canadian-style bacon.

My favorite New Braunfels restaurant, though, is Krause's, operated by a young gourmet with a noble paunch, Kermit Krause. Kermit's prices are as reasonable as those at Grandma and Grandpa Holmes's place, only the food is more German-style.

Krause's is a good place for breakfast. There's smoky, peppered bacon, cured in the premises. And Kermit Krause is a genius at concocting hot sauces, which are always on the table and are recommended with scrambled eggs if you have a good constitution.

The ling is a giant food fish of the cod family.

I've suggested to the Norsemen of Bosque County that if they ever have trouble getting lutefisk from Norway they should contract Paul Santerre of Galveston to supply them with his delicious version of barbecued ling.

Mr. Santerre is the owner of my favorite restaurant on Galveston Island, called the Golden Greek, and he is a very imaginative chef. When there's a big ling catch off the island, the Golden Creek always gets a lot of ling steaks and barbecues them. And the ling which comes out of the barbecue pit tastes very much like the finest of Alaskan smoked salmon.

The best place for oysters along the Texas Gulf Coast was Kelley's Bar in Houston, across Texas Avenue from the Rice Hotel. It closed in 1972 to make way for another bank.

You sidled up to the tile bar with a footrail. And a team of oyster-shucking virtuosos was ready to serve you. Deftly they broke open the hinged double shells with thrusts of short knives into the interior regions of the bivalve. Then they offered up on tin plates those soul-satisfying products of the sea's chemistry, tasting as if they were new from the Gulf of Mexico.

"The oyster she got muscle in her mantle and the oyster she is stubborn," said John Escamillo, the elder statesman of Kelly's Bar shuckers. "You get on wrong side of the oyster and push and you got knife in your hand. Only a short knife will stand the pressure. It takes a special knife. We get our knives from New Orleans and from Nassau."

John Escamillo, a big Indian originally from Laredo, said that about 7,200 oysters were opened at Kelley's on an average day.

Wheeling along the river road near the adobe village of San Elizario in El Paso County, Tom Diamond and I saw a sign, "San Elizario Bakery — Asaderos Frescos." We were pleasantly surprised that a bakery on the U.S. side of the Rio Grande should be selling asaderos frescos, the wonderful Chihuahua-style cheese made famous in the village of Ahumada, Mexico.

This ropy, pungent cheese is sold thin-sliced and in a round shape to fit packages in which tortillas are merchandised. And the cheese is particularly used as a baked topping for enchiladas suizas.

The best catfish I've eaten were raised in the Kirschberg (Cherry Mountain) community near Fredericksburg, Texas. On the Kirschberg catfish farm you can often see forty thousand or more fish swimming around in filtered, oxygenated, and temperature-controlled fresh spring water. And the fish are eating foods recommended by scientists and are listening to "environmental" music piped through underwater speakers.

"Do catfish really seem to enjoy soothing-type music?" I asked Forrest Arnke, manager of the farm on Cherry Mountain.

"Seem to," he said, and added: "In early spring the females lay their eggs in man-made containers. The eggs are then placed in incubators, hatched, and then raised in the spring water with music by Muzak. The environment in which these fish are grown and the food they eat are such that at the market place the fish have no detectable odor."

From the minute they are processed until they're in nearby Fredericksburg restaurants the fish are kept at a temperature of 33°F (never frozen) and served fresh soon after processing.

Pittsburg, a town of about five thousand in an inspirational setting of pine and hardwood forests and many groves of peach trees, calls itself "The Hot Links Capital of Texas." You won't find hot links, which are very spicy sausages, served on Pittsburg's main street, which is quite crooked. (The crookedness of the main street is traced to early days' lazy ways: in the 1850s a big tree fell down and caused a detour which has continued to this day.)

The places to get hot links are two establishments called Warwick's and Potter's on Market and Marshall Streets in the downtown section. Warwick's has tables and booths, but the drive-in window seems the most popular, and I think that Pittsburg's version of hot sausages are best if taken home and browned on a grill.

Potter's has plank tables and benches.

Fellow named Charley Hasselback made the first of the Pittsburg-type hot links sometime back in the nineteenth century. They're inexpensive — four for twenty-nine cents the last time I bought some at Potter's.

Port Arthur is called "The Cajun Capital of Texas" because it has so many inhabitants originally from the French-speaking parishes of southwestern Louisiana. Probably the best Cajun-style food in Port Arthur is served at a café called Leo and Willie's, operated by Leo and Willie Hebert. The accent, of course, is on crayfish dishes in season, fresh crayfish coming in daily from Breaux Bridge in Louisiana. I had another specialty of the house, barbecued crab claws, which was very good, although you need a towel after you get through breaking the shells covering the succulent meat just above the pincers.

Leo Hebert said that barbecued crab claws "isn't exactly a Cajun dish. I think a fellow we called Old Man Granger (I don't remember his name) originated barbecued crab claws long ago at his little café in Sabine Pass."

20. "The Chili Prayer"

"Chili eaters is some of Your chosen people. We don't know why You so doggone good to us."

Bones Hooks
speaking to God

When I started this book, I aimed for it to be only about chili con carne. Then I decided that some "companion" native foods of the Southwest deserved places in these chronicles.

Still, this book was mainly written in the blessed hope that chili con carne, especially that composed in the old Texas way, shall not vanish from this earth.

As mentioned in an early chapter, going to town on Saturday night and having a bowl of red at a small café became a ritual in the Southwest by the 1890s. Later, when Mama learned to make it, Saturday night chili became a regular thing in thousands of Southwest homes.

"My mother always cooked it in a deep old black skillet, and you could smell it all afternoon, and you practically died," said one Dallas native who now lives in New York City. "Now, for me, chili is all entwined with memories of home."

"Saturday night chili kept our family together," said Willie Schliepake, a member of the clan who operated Texas' oldest

178

continuously operated restaurant, and one of the best, the Blue Front in Dallas. "Mama always made two big pots of chili on Saturday. One was mild-flavored for her and the girls. One was full of mischief, with little red slivers of chili peppers all mixed up in the meat, for Pap and me.

"Those pots kept us home on Saturday nights — at least, we weren't about to do any prowling until way after supper was over. And Mama saved enough so we could have chili in the scrambled eggs for breakfast Sunday mornings. I always jumped out of bed early on Sunday mornings."

This book will close with a "chili prayer." It was spoken at a reunion of old-time cowhands. Matthew (Bones) Hooks said the prayer.

Bones Hooks was the most beloved of the pioneer black range cooks (he was also a great cowboy) in the Texas Panhandle. When I was a shirttail kid in the 1920s, Bones was an old man and a patient of a medical doctor relative of mine, R. D. Gist of Amarillo. Dr. Gist told me it was a pleasure to treat the wise old cowboy.

"I collected handsome fees from Bones," said Dr. Gist. "He paid me off by cooking big pots of chili, the best I've ever eaten."

What Hooks called his "flower tradition" had nothing to do with chili con carne, but it should be mentioned. He came up into the Panhandle from East Texas in the early 1880s on his mule, Dinamite (Hooks's spelling), and there was no more popular man on the range. This wasn't just because of his prowess as a cowpuncher or his superlative cooking.

Bones worked hard at being a friend. When he heard that one of the cowboys he knew had been hurt or was ill, and when the prairies were in flower, Bones would bring or send a bunch of wild blossoms to his friend.

The "flower tradition" started when Bones learned that a white cowboy named Tommy Clayton had been grievously injured in a fall from a horse down in the Pecos country. "I had rode with Tommy a lot," said Bones. The black range cook was in the Panhandle and he couldn't leave in the midst of a roundup. So he gathered some flowers and sent them by another cowboy, who was riding south.

Tommy Clayton was dead and the flowers were wilted when the messenger arrived. The flowers were put on Clayton's grave. "And they were almost another funeral when I finally got down in the Pecos River rangelands and seen Tommy's folks," said Hooks. "Tommy's people sure appreciated them flowers."

After that, Bones gave hundreds of bouquets of wild-flowers to ailing cowboys, white flowers when he could find them. He said this signified his love for his white friends.

At this old cowboys' reunion in Amarillo, Bones said his "chili prayer." He had cooked a huge pot of chili con carne. Everyone was anxious to get at it. But Hooks had a deep reverence for good chili. Before it was dished out, he got on his knees and bowed his head. The other old cowpunchers just bowed their heads. Most of them were too stove up to get on their knees. Bones's prayer went something like this:

"Lord God, You know us old cowhands is forgetful. Sometimes, I can't even recollect what happened yestiddy. We *is* forgetful. We just know daylight and dark, summer, fall, winter, and spring. But I sure hope we don't never forget to thank You before we is about to eat a mess of good chili.

"We don't know why, in Your wisdom, You been so dog-gone good to us. The heathen Chinese don't have no chili, ever. The Frenchmens is left out. The Rooshians don't know no more about chili than a hog does about a sidesaddle. Even the Meskins don't get a good whiff of it unless they stay around here.

"Chili eaters is some of Your chosen people. We don't know why You so doggone good to us. But, Lord God, don't never think we ain't grateful for this chili we about to eat. Amen."